FOR BEN

I will choose you for the rest of my life. Thank you for choosing me back and for always choosing the high road, the right way, and God's best for our family. I love you.

To Jesus

Even while I was still a sinner, You chose to die for me. You have provided all of us with the greatest example of love known to mankind.

CONTENTS

HOW TO USE THIS CURRICULUM

This curriculum can be used in a small group, as a couple, or as an individual.
Each week is designed to be self-explanatory in terms of questions and content.
The goal of this study is to create unity through personal responsibility. This is a versatile study and the learning can be achieved in multiple ways.

Small Group Leaders
Each week contains reading, scripture, and questions to facilitate conversation. Prayerfully consider each week how the discussion would be best approached. This may include remaining as a large group, having couples find a space by themselves to share with each other, or a combination of both.

Here are some helpful tips for a successful study:
1. Create a relaxed environment
2. Set the tone that this is a place for sharing, not a place for open conflict
3. Read each week thoroughly before the group arrives
4. Pray over each participant
5. Encourage, but do not force, sharing or participation
6. Encourage couples to continue the conversation all week

Couples
This study can easily be completed in the privacy of your home and relationship. In reading through the weeks and exercises together, you can encourage dialogue in your marriage, and put into practice the principles you are reading.

A few ground rules:
1. Commit to a distraction free environment
2. Decide that no matter how difficult or sensitive the subject matter, you will respectfully communicate toward breakthrough
3. Pray together as a couple
4. Focus on your growth, and take responsibility for your contribution
5. Have fun—let this content inspire you to new places in your marriage

Individuals
Perhaps you've decided to read and study this material on your own without your spouse. Perfectly fine. As the author, most of the decisions I made to choose my spouse were made alone. I decided the type of spouse I wanted to be and chose to become that without a lot of discussion. The key is not to impose what you are learning on your spouse. Do not suddenly require new behaviors, new conversation, or new attitudes. You're choosing to choose them and that can be done silently. You are not choosing new behaviors for them. At the right time, in the right place, perhaps you could begin the conversation around what you're learning, or allow your spouse to see the changes in you. Taking responsibility for how you show up in your marriage is a great gift to your spouse and yourself.

INTRODUCTION

A thriving marriage is within the reach of two willing people. If you're reading this, you're either currently married or headed toward wedded bliss. This study is intended to serve you as you build a marriage over a lifetime. Everyone wants to be chosen, whether for a kickball team in elementary school or as a lifelong spouse. Choosing a spouse is not about making one choice on one special day, but rather communicating the power of that choice to your spouse daily. It will speak to their heart: "I chose you. I choose you daily. And I will choose you again."

My hope is that you may experience the great gift of a healthy marriage and that you can be the type of spouse that we all aspire to become—a giving one. No matter how long you've been together, I know that your greatest days are ahead of you. The lessons in this book are hard won, and not a theory. Over twenty years, I've had the privilege and the pain of my choices, both the good and the bad. When I fully surrendered my choices to Christ, and the good of my spouse, I've watched the fruit of joy, peace, and unity grow in my marriage. I didn't know that a marriage rich with purpose, love, and trust was possible until now.

Cheering for you,
Melissa Pierce

I CHOOSE YOU PROMISE

I chose you on our wedding day.

I choose you today and every day.

I choose to prioritize your needs.

I choose to listen to your perspective.

I choose to let down my guard.

I choose to make God the center of our lives.

I choose to respect your personhood.

I choose to die to our differences.

I choose to champion your dreams.

I choose to walk through valleys and fire and pain with you.

I choose to celebrate with you on the mountaintops.

I choose to know you more intimately.

I choose to care for you deeply.

I choose to protect your heart.

I choose to become the partner you always dreamed of having.

I promise to make daily decisions that remind you that you have been chosen by me.

I chose you. I choose you daily. And I will choose you again.

OUR STORY

Ben and I chose each other for life on August 4th, 2001. I was barely twenty-two, and he, just twenty-four. As of the time of this writing, we will have been married for over twenty years. For the past nine years, we have worked together in our chosen vocation. When you work together on a daily basis, marriage begins to feel like it is measured in dog years. So, mathematically speaking, Ben and I have been married for one hundred and forty years. Like many at the beginning of their marriage, we didn't know what we did not know. Nor did we anticipate the number of lessons that lay before us. Marriage became a mirror that reflected the health of our souls, and as we observed the reflection through our treatment of each other, we recognized the opportunities for growth, health, and change.

We were equally willing. We were not equally perfect, and our families of origin were largely different. As the author of this book, I'm sharing our story, but only from my perspective. Harnessing the power of choice has been my own journey within the context of our marriage. So, the stories you'll read will be about my pathology. Be sure of it, Ben has his own, but I told him to get his own book. I rightfully take much of the responsibility for the difficulty and conflict in the early days of our marriage. I trusted no one, and worse, I didn't trust myself to begin the journey toward trust.

When I took my vows, I had not closely observed one healthy marriage in my lifetime. As a kid, sitcoms were my window into the functional. I imagined what it would be like for parents to speak to each other respectfully, solve problems mutually, give attention to their children generously, and laugh along the way—all in the space of thirty minutes. Even unconventional families like Full House seemed to make life work well. In the early 90's, TGIF filled me with family aspirations beyond anything I have previously observed. Simply, I wanted to be them.

Whether it was those families on TV or something else, Ben and I made a commitment. We did not just want our marriage to work—we wanted it to thrive. That kind of mindset cleared the path for every step that followed. In essence, even when I didn't know how to take the next step, I tried to discern the next right action. Incrementally, choosing wisely created enough peace, respect, and civility to discuss the deeper issues. If we were fighting, the next right action was to reconcile and thoroughly resolve the issue. Make no mistake, our marriage has not been easy. Even so, these past twenty years have been rich. Our single marital advantage is that we both wholeheartedly believe that anything, and perhaps everything we intend to do is possible. This state of mind is not one we adopted to help our marriage. Rather, we're both hardwired as hyper optimists. If change was necessary, it was possible and probable. And it was me that had to change.

The change that was necessary was not simply righting my bad behavior, but a process of discovery, personal responsibility, and healing which yielded change. I had to initiate the process of healing, and yet the healing itself could not happen in isolation. I needed and still need people, books, blogs, podcasts, counselors, and most importantly, Jesus.

I grew up in chaos. I had to find a way to peace.
I grew up with no model of forgiveness or resolution. I find reliable and godly ones.
I grew up in a home with no stable center. I wanted to exude consistency.
I grew up in a home with no boundaries. I have tried to be respectful of others.

I had intellectual knowledge of the right choices, as most of us do. I lacked the emotional maturity, the positive role models, and the healthy soul to build the marriage I desired.

I was desperate for better. I decided to rely on simple wisdom.

"If I do something good, perhaps I'll get something good." That is in alignment with the Scripture:

"Whatever a man sows, that he will also reap." (Gal. 6:7b NKJV)

My choice began at the atomic level.

I decided if I became mad, frustrated, or hurt, I was going to take responsibility for managing my negative emotions appropriately.

If I had hurt Ben, I was going to swallow my pride and choose to apologize and seek his forgiveness.

I quickly learned that the tiny shifts in my heart mattered. I started to believe that the seemingly minor, but negative thoughts running through my head were consequential, and that I could indeed control my attitude, tongue, and mood.

As we approached each obstacle, we had to choose either our individual preference or the greater good of our spouse. So far, we've been choosing each other.

I wish I could tell you that our journey toward choosing each other was filled with thirty minutes of sitcom-worthy solutions and jokes. I cannot.

I can tell you consistency is key. By consistently making choices to work on myself, surrender to God's word, learn from others, and communicate in respectful ways, marriage has become an enjoyable partnership.

The First Ten Years

The first ten years of our marriage were both good and bad. I came with baggage—and not a tiny carry-on. I came with a truckload of wounds, pain, and mistrust, all stemming from a childhood of poverty and abuse. Once the honeymoon was over, the honeymoon was decidedly over. The real us emerged. I was very sensitive to change, which meant I was controlling. If we had a plan, and there was any deviation from the plan, I could not handle it. I would become angry and frustrated. There was a lot of silent treatment, leaving Ben to figure out what to do next. Real talk, I was painfully immature.

I was also absorbed in my pain and in myself. I was not fully in touch with how my mood swings, sensitivities, and harsh reactions affected Ben. My commitment to my preferences for meals, plans, outings, and time with people made it hard to respect and listen to his desires. During the first ten years of marriage, we probably did 90 percent of what I wanted to do, 90 percent of the time. Ben is incredibly fun, with loads of fantastic ideas that are consistently better than mine. Sometimes, I think about the things we possibly missed out on because of my smallness. Ben, if you're reading this, I'm sorry all over again.

My heart was like a difficult knot, with all of the pain and the wounds tangled up with the aspirations, hopes, desires, and knowledge of God's way. Like with any good knot, I began to dig at it a little at a time, coming at it from different angles, hoping to find the string that would give way and make it untangle.

Little by little, I began to transform. I created the conflict, but I also worked hard to resolve it. I knew my anger was harmful, but I didn't know what to do about it or how to control it. I craved resolution. When I would blow up, I would always ask Ben to forgive me. I would explain that I was truly sorry and that I would work on changing. I had choices to make.

The change I sought was within my grasp. Would I choose to lay hold of that better, more loving approach to my spouse?

Life was not this difficult daily. We had a lot of fun, enjoyed being around each other, and shared common interests and goals. We traveled, were successful in our careers, and had a lot of reasons to be happy. Neither of us would describe this period of our marriage as dreadful or teetering on the edge of divorce. If this determination and vision for a better marriage were not on my horizon, we would have almost certainly begun a death spiral. Though it was tenuous, and my mood was unpredictable, we both had a deep desire for our marriage to work. We were solidly committed to each other, and we were in love, but learning how to more highly value each other.

I recognized in my worst moments that I didn't even want to be around me, so why would anyone else? And through the gentle leadership of the Holy Spirit, I was living far below God's intention for a beautiful marriage. It was then that I made the decision that I was going to GROW in my respect for Ben. No matter what it took, I was going to treat him with the highest level of kindness and learn to subject my emotions to my will and the word of God. It was this posture of heart and action-oriented focus that took a good marriage, albeit fraught with issues, and made it great. It's likely that my heart change developed because of Ben's example. He always treated me well. I can count on one hand the number of times Ben has become angry with me or treated me disrespectfully.

He has been the most loving human example I have ever known. I could not be more grateful.

Around the ten-year mark, my trust in Ben and the strength of our marriage became deeper. I began to relax, stop bristling, and put down my armor.

So, here is what I did. I accepted Proverbs 18:20: "Death and life are in the power of the tongue, And those who love it will eat its fruit." I took that literally, as I do with the rest of the Bible, and I began to say what I wanted to be. While I had trouble controlling some of my behaviors, I could control repeating scripture or making statements about who and what I wanted to become. It was free, and I could start immediately. In the privacy of my home, I began speaking specific Scripture over myself and marriage consistently, daily, sometimes a hundred or maybe a thousand times per day.

Romans 12:2 tells us we can be "transformed by the renewing of [our] mind." Transformed means to change into another form. This does not mean you'll become your alter ego, like Beyoncé to Sasha Fierce, but rather renewing your mind transforms you in such a way that you reflect the image of Christ. Through confessing Scripture, I did not become a Jesus robot—thinking, acting and being exactly the same as my Christian siblings. Instead, this act of choosing God's word as my foundation of truth has helped me to live my best married life and my best life overall. I can look back over the past twenty years and I can wholeheartedly say that I am a better version of myself because of the transforming power of God's word.

What happens next?

As I healed, I became less selfish, which made me more sensitive to Ben's dreams and desires. It was like I had been emotionally deaf, and I could finally hear for the first time. This was a pivotal time, as my growth intersected with a long-held goal of Ben's. He always wanted to build a house. I had zero understanding of what that meant and honestly no paradigm for buying or building a home. In their thirty-eight years of marriage, my parents never owned a home. To Ben, home means roots and permanence—the likes of which I had never experienced.

Building a home was so far outside of the realm of my comprehension that I always dismissed it, negated its possibility, and stalled. After twelve years of marriage, we needed to make a move thirty minutes north closer to the church we had started. We began searching for a home, or even a plot of land. One day, as we were driving around seeking a little slice of paradise, it happened. We found a piece of land that we both loved. We took the plunge and made the purchase. Buying an empty lot can be relatively easy. Building a house is another matter entirely. This project was a big deal and a big step. If you've ever built a house, you know it takes fortitude and financial responsibility. I had the former, but not yet the latter. We had done a lot to prepare, but I had trouble living inside of a budget. One day Ben was reviewing our finances and suddenly, I heard him quietly say to himself, "We're never going to be able to build this house."

It was a defeated whisper, and it broke my heart.

Five years prior, my heart would not have been broken. I was too selfish, too deaf, too wounded, and too immature to understand the needs and desires of my partner. But my determination to choose Ben over the pain of my past put me in a position to legitimately hear and understand his pain and then respond.

Ben's pain became my pain, and I chose to change my spending habits. I'll spare you the details of my frugality, but I went into crazy, insane, gazelle-intense Dave Ramsey Baby Steps mode. My willingness to change and champion Ben's desire developed new levels of trust, communication, partnership, and intimacy. We were able to build our house, and Ben was able to fulfill his lifelong dream. This is just one story that illustrates the power of choice. My biggest lesson is that tiny choices are what dreams are made of.

Managing my heart finally mattered. The moments I chose to end an argument I had probably started, to seek forgiveness and reconciliation, to reduce my silent treatment time, or to grow in my respect and love for Ben finally added up to something tangible. A house was a giant project, but one that meant something to the person who means the most to me. Ben, I know you're reading this, and you're welcome.

In reflection, I understand that the power of choice fueled the power to change. The next right choice began to build, one upon another, until our marriage hit positive tipping point upon positive tipping point in various areas of our lives.

Over the past twenty years, I've discovered that choice is a great gift from God. It is a power to steward a reservoir of ability available to us all equally.

Equal circumstances? Ha. You would not choose my starting point.
Equal talent? No way. I have no specific skills.
Equal opportunity? Probably not.
Equal knowledge? There are a lot of people who are much smarter than me.

Equal power to choose? Absolutely.

The next right choice, no matter how difficult, is available to everyone.

When things don't come easy, we still have the power of choice.

Every human has a heart, a mind, and a soul. We have God-given decision-making faculties that, if leveraged appropriately, will send us in the direction we ultimately desire.

That is what this book is about. It's about recognizing that when choice is all you've got, that's fine, because choice is all you need. When you choose to love, honor, and serve your spouse, you're honoring God by rightly using what He has given you.

If you're considering whether choice-making can create a positive difference in your marriage, I'll share this:

I have no regrets, no shame, and no embarrassment for every moment I have made a better choice. I'm proud of every argument I stopped, every instance of forgiveness and reconciliation, and the loving union I've worked to build.

I do, however, regret my selfish choices. I regret flying off the handle, being angry over very little thing, and wasting precious time detailing the finer points of my argument.

Take note, I said nothing of my spouse's reciprocation. I didn't tell you the story of how Ben suddenly became even more perfect and began to choose me, and now every day is a "choose-off" to determine who can be the most giving. I learned quickly that my choices are not about him, but they are for him. Choosing wisely is about me. Often, we see marriage as a seesaw of getting and giving. The power of choice is the power to choose to be giving. Getting will come, sure. Your needs will be met by your partner. But the real gift—the actual blessing—is in the personal transformation that will take place in you.

Nowadays, we do 90 percent of what Ben wants to do, 90 percent of the time. He was playing the long game, knowing that an unselfish choice today creates a good result tomorrow, as he always does, and I have learned to do that along with him.

The choice is yours. My deepest desire is that this book inspires you to choose your way to a thriving marriage.

What choices are right in front of you?

Respond

How would you describe your marriage?

1. On the brink?
2. Decent, but needs work?
3. Better than average, but still striving?
4. Thriving?

_____

_____

_____

_____

_____

_____

_____

_____

_____

_____

_____

_____

_____

_____

_____

_____

Week One

THE POWER OF BEING CHOSEN

Week One
THE POWER OF BEING CHOSEN

How would you describe the feeling of being chosen?

Travel back to grade school. It's a hot and sunny day on the ball field at school, and your PE teacher has decided upon a friendly game of kickball. To everyone's horror, he states that two students will be choosing teams. He picks the two most athletic kids in the class to be "captains," and the slow torture begins.

Suddenly, the eight-year-old cortisol levels everywhere begin to rise. Everyone stands taller and attempts to appear tougher than usual. You can sense the tension and the anticipation of the inevitable. The ultimate schoolyard rejection is coming, and everybody knows it. Somebody is going to be picked last. The captains begin with their friends first. Everyone can relate to that—gotta show love to the tribe. Then the jocks get picked. You rationalize that one too. Then, the popular kids with no distinct athletic qualities are chosen. Your face is now red with embarrassment. The bottom of the barrel is quickly approaching, and every insecurity you have is roaring loudly in your head. As the pressure is mounting, you and the remaining few silently pray, "Please God, don't let me get picked last."

Suddenly, a voice: "God, is that you?" Then, shaken from your invocation of the Almighty, you hear that glorious sound—your name.

You were picked. They picked you.

You were chosen, and you weren't last!

As you walk away from the line of remaining losers, you can't help but feel a pang of pity. You know exactly how they feel. You wish you could address their pain. Instead, you rush to the safety of your new best buddies. Your teammates! The joy you feel is indescribable—the rush of adrenaline and all the happy brain chemicals flood your system. Immediately, the world is a better place to be. You now have the refuge of your people. It is only grade school kickball, but still, they chose you.

All of us have been there.
Every single one of us has experienced this internal question of worthiness.
Am I worthy of being picked, selected, chosen?

Do I add something valuable enough to be seen?

You're married, so you have experienced the joy of being chosen for life. But in our marriages, this semi-traumatic kickball example plays out day after day.

Like the lineup of our third-grade classmates, we have a lineup of priorities—all kinds of things demanding they be chosen first. Important things like work and business, spiritual life, finances, schedules, kids and their education, our personal needs, and our spouse vie for attention. All worthy, all necessary. All cannot be chosen at once. Our selections must be carefully prioritized to correctly communicate the true intentions of our hearts.

In the lineup of priorities, where does your spouse rank? After your spiritual relationship with God, is your spouse your immediate next?

We can too comfortably rely on the big choice that happened on the big day to continue to speak for us long after the honeymoon is over. The colossal decision to choose a partner for life is wonderful, but it will not sustain your marriage daily. Reinforcing your big choice with small, consistent choices to prioritize your spouse will invigorate and sustain your relationship.

Too often, our spouse is chosen last. How do our priorities communicate to our spouse? Is our spouse regularly waiting, hoping they are picked before work, self-improvement, immaturity, and our selfish desires?

This Study exists to help every married person consistently communicate the following to their husband or wife:

• I fully accept you.
• I prioritize you over important things.
• I value you and will add value to you.
• And so, I choose you over and over again.

The power of choice applied to our marriage is perhaps the greatest tool we have in our marriage tool belt.

Here is the clear and powerful message to send your spouse:

I estimate your worth to be above all others.

In this idea, God is our great example. He chose us. God went to great lengths to communicate His love for us through the combination of acceptance, value, and prioritization.

He wants us to know and understand that He exercised the power of choice. He was not forced to do anything for us. He chose to give His only Son to us, and that makes the reality of His love even greater.

All praise to God, the Father of our Lord Jesus Christ, who has blessed us with every spiritual blessing in the heavenly realms because we are united with Christ. Even before he made the world, God loved us and chose us in Christ to be holy and without fault in his eyes. God decided in advance to adopt us into his own family by bringing us to himself through Jesus Christ. This is what he wanted to do, and it gave him great pleasure. So we praise God for the glorious grace he has poured out on us who belong to his dear Son. He is so rich in kindness and grace that he purchased our freedom with the blood of his Son and forgave our sins. He has showered his kindness on us, along with all wisdom and understanding. (Ephesians 1:3–8 NLT, emphasis the author's)

In this passage, Paul details God's choice:

1. God chooses to always be kind and generous to us
2. God chooses to forgive us and always sees the best in us
3. God chooses to sacrifice for us
4. God chooses to communicate commitment

KIND AND GENEROUS

What would happen in your marriage if you made an intentional effort to be kind to your spouse? Not cordial or civil or mildly pleasant, but intentionally and meaningfully and consistently kind?

List specific ways you might be more kind to your husband or wife?

Examples could include:

1. Using encouraging words
2. Taking notice of your spouse's effort
3. Framing requests and questions in ways that are easy to hear

_____

_____

_____

_____

_____

What would happen in your marriage if you were generous toward your spouse, both tangibly and intangibly? A tangible instance could include a small gift. Intangibles can be generous gestures of giving grace, and serving them in unexpected, but meaningful ways.

List specific examples of how you might be more generous with your spouse.

Be extravagantly generous with grace. We can be so generous when friends or colleagues are late, make a mistake, or do something wrong. Yet with our spouse we can be so stingy. Ben is generous with grace, and that is why I love him so. He never gives me the cold shoulder or a wall of irritation. He just accepts that I make mistakes. He is generous.

_____

_____

_____

_____

_____

FORGIVENESS AND ENCOURAGEMENT

What would happen in your marriage if conflicts were resolved thoroughly, and forgiveness was expressed openly?

_____

_____

_____

_____

_____

What would happen in your marriage if you became your spouse's biggest cheerleader? What if you constantly called out the greatness inside of them? What if you always chose to see the best in them?

What would you need to change to make this a reality?

_____

_____

_____

_____

_____

SACRIFICIAL POSTURE

What would happen in your marriage if you sought out ways to sacrifice for the good of your spouse or your marriage? List ways you can begin to occasionally sacrifice your preferences.

_____

_____

_____

_____

_____

COMMUNICATE COMMITMENT

What would happen in your marriage if you verbally reinforced your commitment to each other? How might your spouse benefit from knowing that you are safe, stable, and steady? What needs to take place in your own heart?

_____

_____

_____

_____

_____

Survive, Thrive, and Someplace in Between

Whether you are barely surviving in your marriage or already thriving, these principles will enhance, and possibly transform, your life and your marriage. One thing is certain: a thriving marriage is no accident. It is the product of intentional and willing people ready to make daily choices that demonstrate their love for each other, to get uncomfortable with the marital status quo, and accept the challenge to grow into the spouse they committed to be on their wedding day.

Respond

This Week's Homework:

Choosing Your Spouse:

1. Pray: Make time to pray for them and with them.
2. Ask: How can I choose you today?
3. Grow: Work on an area of your life that will please your spouse.
4. No: What things can you say no to that come before your marriage?

Healthy Priority Structure:

1. God
2. Marriage
3. Family (including children or extended family, if you have them)
4. Vocation: School, Business, Work
5. Serving in the community or Hobbies, Recreation, Fun, Self-Improvement, Individual Projects

Along with your spouse, evaluate your priorities:

1. Where do we spend too much time?
2. What can we stop doing?
3. What should we start doing?
4. Where can we invest our time for greater returns in the future?

" **HERE IS THE CLEAR AND POWERFUL MESSAGE TO SEND YOUR SPOUSE: I ESTIMATE YOUR WORTH TO BE ABOVE ALL OTHERS.**

Journal

Week Two

THE POWER TO CHANGE

Week Two
THE POWER TO CHANGE

Choice is perhaps the singular most distinctive trait of the human race. We hold a power that no other species is able to wield. We are empowered to choose how we behave and who we are. Every day we make choices about everything from our coffee, to our identity, to our behavior.

I don't like what I'm wearing. I can choose to change it. He loves trying new things. He is free to seek adventure. You prefer lattes over cappuccinos. You're the boss.

We desire a thriving marriage. It's no accident.

You are endowed with the power to choose and therefore blessed with the power to change.

#blessed

Growing up in the nineties, we had no hashtags. The hashtag is the artist formerly known as the pound sign and was used on phones that stayed inside of our homes. We had no social media and no way to measure likes. Yet even without Instagram, we still knew who was popular and who was not. I was not.

I never seemed to fit in exactly. I was social and I had some friends, but I had no definable group. I had a looming sense of awkwardness which made fitting into a group, well, awkward. I didn't know I was a misfit then. But now, through reflection, I can see it all clearly. Because of being a misfit, I struggled hard, and that is why I am #blessed.

My misfit status was partially due to my parents' dysfunction. They were not social and did not teach me how to be social or model socially acceptable behaviors. I rarely participated in an activity outside of school and was not exposed to the same things as other kids. I knew I wanted more in life, and I also knew it would not naturally flow to me. I was instinctively aware that many of the odds for the life I wanted were stacked squarely and firmly against me.

The available tool—my personal secret weapon—was my power to choose.

Perhaps you relate to my story, and you can also say:

I don't fit in. Well, show up anyway.
I've got insecurity and fear and my obnoxious inner critic telling me I'm not good enough. You can choose to show up anyway.
I didn't have the same resources. Work hard to earn them and show up anyway.
I wasn't afforded a seat at the table. So, build one and show up anyway.

Struggle has blessed me with the tenacity and capacity to choose and choose again.

I've always viewed choice as hope. I can remember moments as a girl when I vowed that I would make different choices than my parents. Early on, I adopted a keen awareness through daily observation that bad choices equal bad results and good choices equal better results. Groundbreaking, I know.

I was desperate for hope that life could be better, easier, more enjoyable, and frankly worth living. I put my eggs in the basket of choice and have found that consistently choosing well has given me the life I was seeking.

Pain and Choice, Choice and Pain

Why is it so hard to choose correctly all the time? Because long-term choices cause us short-term pain, and short-term choices cause us long-term pain.

There it is, that word. Pain. We spend so much of our lives avoiding or alleviating pain.

What if persevering through pain is the path toward the marriage and life of your dreams? Or better, the God-intended life of fullness and abundance.

In relationships, it's the pain of humility, the pain of apology, the pain of surrender, and ultimately the pain of change for the good of your partner.

Comfort in the short-term is deceptive and fleeting. Pain on our way to progress is a friend and a gift.

We repel pain. We rebuke pain. We can't stand pain. Anything but more pain. You might be thinking, I'm doing this study because I want to stop the pain, numb the pain, and address the pain. You're telling me there is more pain?

Pain is and will always be involved. So, choose your pain.

In the context of your marriage, this looks like deciding whether to be snarky now and release the nukes or hold your tongue and wait until you can be rational and kind. It may seem more gratifying to be rude in the moment, but it will only serve to bring a divide, creating more work to rebuild the intimacy, trust, and love you truly desire.

"But the fruit of the Spirit is love, joy, peace, longsuffering, kindness, goodness, faithfulness, gentleness [and] self-control. Against such [things] there is no law." (Galatians 5:22–23 NKJV, emphasis the author's)

When we choose short-term comfort, we only compound future pain. When we choose short-term pain (humility, gentleness, self-control) we compound long-term comfort.

Respond

What can I change that will likely be painful in the short-term but beneficial in the long-term?

_____

Who will benefit the most if I make these choices?

Kids (if you have them) _____

Spouse _____

You _____

What could the future look like if you don't make these necessary changes and choices?

_____

You might be saying: "I've tried this before and I did not see a difference."

Yes, ok, I've been there too. This week is about unselfish action that will hopefully have a positive impact on your marriage, and it's also about transforming into an unselfish and giving individual. My hope is that you would move from choosing well to being well—to recognizing that you are on a personal growth journey with shared consequences.

Usually, the choices we make don't create an immediate difference. It is what we do over time that creates outcomes.

Your health tells the story of your diet and exercise over time, not after one meal. Your finances tell the story of your budgeting, spending, and discipline over a year.

Our choices tell the story of our deeply held values. We sometimes meet frustration in the middle of our current reality and aspirations. Our consistent choices tell us who we are today, and our aspirations point us toward who we'd like to become.

I find the Bible to be my highest ideal. I encourage you to align your marriage aspirations with God's word and then determine that is who you are.

Respond

Question: Do my consistent choices align with my long-term aspirations? (circle one)

Yes
Maybe
No
Sometimes

It is freeing to be honest with ourselves about our choices today and our aspirations for tomorrow. We sometimes confuse our aspirations with our daily choices and end up lying to ourselves about what we are doing and how we well are stewarding the gifts and resources in our lives.

The way we know the difference between our choices and aspirations is to inventory our behavior.

What have I been choosing in my marriage?
1. _____
2. _____
3. _____

Who do I aspire to be in my marriage and for my spouse?
1. _____
2. _____
3. _____

What choices are necessary to become what I truly desire to be?

When your choices are consistently in alignment with your aspirations, you're walking the path that leads to where you ultimately want to go. There may be obstacles, but at least you're no longer wandering.

We can't do God's part, and He won't do our part.

Scripture to meditate on:

> I call heaven and earth as witnesses today against you, that I have set before you life and death, blessing and cursing; therefore choose life, that both you and your descendants may live; that you may love the Lord your God, that you may obey His voice, and that you may cling to Him, for He is your life and the length of your days; and that you may dwell in the land which the Lord swore to your fathers, to Abraham, Isaac, and Jacob, to give them.
> (Deuteronomy 30:19–20 NKJV, emphasis the author's)

Choices help you get to know yourself, and those choices tell the story of what you deeply value.

How do you take care of your health and relationships?
How do you choose to spend and steward money?
How do you invest in yourself and others?

Specifically in marriage:
1. How do you speak to your spouse?
2. Do you actively prioritize their wants and needs?
3. Evaluate the quality of treatment you give to your spouse.
4. Do you encourage them regularly?

Choices become habits, which become a lifestyle. Choice reminds us that we can either talk about it or be about it. Choice is the ultimate accountability partner. The opposite of choice is victimization. A victim mentality is a harmful mentality. In the Scripture, we never once see God say to anyone, "Make bad choices in bad situations, because it makes sense and I understand."

The potential for a thriving marriage exists when you make good choices on bad days.

We see people throughout the whole of scripture choosing to rise above adversity happening to them or consequences happening because of them.

Here are a few:

Joseph had many unjust and undeserved circumstances, but he chose to be a man of integrity anyway.

David made massive mistakes and chose to move past them and serve the Lord whole-heartedly.

Paul and Silas worshiped God so hard while incarcerated that their chains fell off and the prison door opened up. The point here is that they chose to worship in a difficult moment. The resulting outcome was physical freedom, but their example serves as an excellent metaphor for our spiritual freedom.

Jesus shows us His humanity by voicing His desire to avoid crucifixion, but choosing to die for us anyway.

Life is hard. Being human is hard. When we commit to using the power of choice as the power to change, God's grace inevitably supports us and surrounds us as we do hard things.

"And He said to me, 'My grace is sufficient for you, for My power is made perfect in weakness.' Therefore most gladly I will rather boast in my infirmities, that the power of Christ may rest on me." (2 Corinthians 12:9 NKJV)

Choosing wisely is not easy, especially at first. It goes against the grain of our impulses and desires. Like every muscle, it can be developed and strengthened. The more you choose your spouse, especially in difficult moments, the easier it becomes. This is not because we are awesome logical people. But in our weakness, God's grace supports us, assists us, and leads us toward right. God's grace is better than my strength.

You can be blessed by the struggle:

List one thing you've learned or a way that you have grown in marriage from God's grace and your struggle:

_____

I have the power to choose something better, and I can have something better. We've all heard and likely used the idiom "it takes two to tango." While true, too much emphasis on a thought like this can leave us feeling powerless in the confines of our marriage.

A person cannot truly tango solo. But one person with the drive and desire to influence their marriage positively can make daily choices that radically improve the quality of their relationship and the atmosphere in their home.

You can take responsibility for your marriage. One person taking responsibility for the quality of the union can make a decent marriage better. Two people taking responsibility can make a good marriage great.

You can be a burden lifter, rather than a burden shifter. Victimization is a pervasive evil that aims to slowly erode our power of choice.

The retaliatory spouse has this attitude:

You didn't, so I won't.
You did, so I will.

The responsible spouse:
Whether you did or did not, I will. I choose to be the best version of myself and the best partner, lover, and companion that I can be.

You can be the tone setter in your marriage. You can create a lifestyle of choice-making that communicates worth, care, love, and value to your partner over and over again. Perhaps the first choice you must make is to forgive painful instances that are in your past. Later, you'll learn more about how forgiveness should be a thorough process where the slate is wiped clean.

In order to have a thriving marriage, you may need to make the choice to let some things go, to move past mistakes, to forgive yourself or to grow as an individual.

The choice ahead of you may be to decide that you will re-prioritize your life, make family first, and, in doing so, reap the rewards of a rich and loving life with your spouse.

If you have yet to experience the power of a thriving marriage, the goal of this book is to remind you that you have been endowed with the power of choice and the permission to change.

We all yearn for better. We spend a lot of life making the wrong choices but hoping for the right results.

Choosing to develop a heart to serve your spouse is a critical and foundational step toward the marriage you dream about having.

CHOOSING TO SERVE
John 2:1-11 NLT

2 The next day there was a wedding celebration in the village of Cana in Galilee. Jesus' mother was there, and Jesus and his disciples were also invited to the celebration.
3 The wine supply ran out during the festivities, so Jesus' mother told him, "They have no more wine."
4 "Dear woman, that's not our problem," Jesus replied. "My time has not yet come."
5 But his mother told the servants, "Do whatever he tells you."
6 Standing nearby were six stone water jars, used for Jewish ceremonial washing. Each could hold twenty to thirty gallons.
7 Jesus told the servants, "Fill the jars with water." When the jars had been filled,
8 he said, "Now dip some out, and take it to the master of ceremonies." So, the servants followed his instructions.
9 When the master of ceremonies tasted the water that was now wine, not knowing where it had come from (though, of course, the servants knew), he called the bridegroom over.
10 "A host always serves the best wine first," he said. "Then, when everyone has had

a lot to drink, he brings out the less expensive wine. But you have kept the best until now!"

11 This miraculous sign at Cana in Galilee was the first time Jesus revealed his glory. And his disciples believed in him.

Jesus's first miracle was at the scene of a wedding. They ran out of wine for the guests, and Jesus took ordinary well water and turned it into an expensive fine wine.

All miracles are supernatural acts, but they always serve someone in a very practical way. Maybe you've been praying that God would do something miraculous in your marriage, and the supernatural you are seeking is wrapped up in your personal service to your husband or wife. Serving will transform them and you.

When you make the choice to serve your spouse, like Jesus chose to serve in that wedding, God will take the water of service and turn it into a miracle.

What ordinary act of service can become a miracle in your marriage?

_____

_____

_____

_____

_____

" **WHEN WE CHOOSE SHORT TERM COMFORT, WE ONLY COMPOUND FUTURE PAIN. WHEN WE CHOOSE SHORT TERM PAIN WE COMPOUND LONG TERM COMFORT.**

Journal

Week Three

YOU DO YOU

Week Three
YOU DO YOU

When you make the decision to get married, your life transitions from "you do you" to "we before me."

You're born. You grow up, you begin to date, have some relationships, and now you're married or about to get married. When you got engaged, you were so excited. You started your Pinterest board, bounced around a few thousand hashtag options, and planned all the pre-wedding festivities. Priorities, right?

You had the wedding, your honeymoon, opened the gifts, and sent thank you notes. Now the whirlwind is over and you're home. Together.

Mutual decision-making begins, and you make the transition from singleness to marriedness. Up until now, no matter the seriousness of your dating relationship, you've been your own person, making your own decisions, and doing your own thing.

Now that you're married, it takes two to make a thing go right. Know what I mean?

You may have prepared for marriage, but you're making a jump from the world of you do you to a foreign land called we before me. These worlds are very different—polar opposites, actually.

It's no secret that our world glorifies you. You, and all of your specialness, you and your individuality, you and your unique needs and requirements.

You do you. You have got to be doing 'you,' or else what are you doing?

You do you culture prizes personal preference. You do you culture elevates individuality in a way that makes it challenging to respect others, sacrifice on their behalf, and be a truly giving partner. Because, after all, if it doesn't fit within how I'm doing me that day, then bye Felicia.

The world's version of happiness and fulfillment looks like fiercely defending your right to be all you, all the time.

So then, how can two people be happily married since that marriage is made up of two people who are more committed to me, than we?

In We Before Me Land, people prioritize the health and strength of their union over their individuality. It's a place where people are sacrificial and generous with their spouse. Make no mistake, the Land of We is not a fairy tale of perfection, but a work in progress. People are progressing through service.

In the Land of We, there is order and peace. Ephesians 5 shows us this mutual sense of love, respect, care, and appreciation for each other.

What if there is a better way? In the context of marriage, the Bible's version of a happy and fulfilled life happens when two people become one. The "one flesh" concept is introduced in the book of Genesis and carried through the epistles.

In Genesis, God decides that Adam should not be alone, and so God creates Eve by taking a rib from Adam's side.

When Adam wakes up and sees Eve he says:

> **"This is now bone of my bones, and flesh of my flesh. . .Therefore a man shall leave his father and mother and be joined to his wife, and they shall become one flesh."**
> **(Genesis 2:23–24 NKJV)**

And Jesus continues to confirm this.

"And He answered and said to them, "Have you not read that He who made them at the beginning 'made them male and female,'

and said, 'For this reason a man shall leave his father and mother and be joined to his wife, and the two shall become one flesh'?

So then, they are no longer two but one flesh. Therefore what God has joined together, let not man separate." (Matthew 19:4-6 NKJV emphasis the author's)

In other words, to have the marriage you truly desire, it won't happen with "you do you," and "I'll do me." Having the marriage you deeply desire can't come from just one spouse being the superhero in the relationship. It looks more like:

• You overcoming you
• You submitting you
• You changing you

so that we can be everything we want to be.

We become spiritually tied to our spouse by the covenant of marriage. However, you are still two people with different life stories, perspectives, habits, and viewpoints.

Each of us has deeply held values that make us who we are. In marriage, as we attempt to become one, we may understand intellectually what we are supposed to do. But for most of us, life can feel more like men are from Mars and women are from Venus, as opposed to two people sharing the same existential space. We don't become physically conjoined, so when does the "being one" part make it to our brains and our mouths?

It happens when you comprehend the greater value in the best of you and the best of your spouse coming together.

Two becoming one is multiplication by reduction. Two becoming one will never suggest that one of us is subtracted.

Chefs are also familiar with this concept. In cooking, a reduction is the process of thickening and intensifying the flavor of a liquid mixture such as a soup or sauce by simmering or boiling.

Sounds like marriage, right?

When making a reduction, the impurities rise to the surface and are skimmed away. The needless and the useless boils down to the very best.

Our individual lives are like ingredients for sauce, and marriage is the pot. I bring my unique blend of herbs and spices and he brings his. We live in the pot. Time and life history and work and bills and sex and kids are like heat. The individual ingredients begin to boil and simmer and meld them together. Over time, if we intentionally allow the heat to work, the impurities rise, and we can see them clearly. If we choose correctly, we remove them as we recognize them for what they are.

The boiling and simmering cause the ingredients to become one another, and you cannot know where one ends and the other begins.

Sounds like marriage, right?

When I was first married, I thought I was amazing. No, seriously. I thought I knew a lot. I was fun, happy, and loved life. I tend to have a very high opinion of my opinion.

At the beginning of marriage, we are all a little this way. Through humility, oneness, self-control, and surrender, I am so much better.

I cannot begin to communicate how much better I am since I started listening to Ben, believing he might know something about life, and trusting his judgment. He began listening, believing, and trusting me too. This is marriage. We become an integrated whole. This beautiful and miraculous exchange of the best of one, and the best of the other, comes together to make something extraordinary. This is only possible through multiplication by reduction. Two becoming one.

It is our deeply held values, our habits, our opinion of ourselves, and our perspectives that cause us to hit gridlock. We cannot seem to move forward and appreciate our spouse for who they are, encouraging them to grow at the same time, at their own pace.

During engagement, our differences were exciting. During marriage, our differences can be irritating, creating a sense of frustration, fear, and loss of control.

What is oneness and why do I want that?

Remember: Marriage is we before me

Oneness is achieved when two individuals decide that their shared goals are more important than their differences.

Oneness is achieved when unity is more important than individuality.

Unity in marriage can be defined as two people on one mission.

Oneness is achieved by respecting who your spouse is, seeking to understand them on the deepest level, developing common goals, and working toward achieving them.

Oneness is beautiful. Oneness is not sounding the same, it's sounding together.

"How good and pleasant it is when God's people live together in unity! It is like precious oil poured on the head, running down on the beard, running down on Aaron's beard, down on the collar of his robe. It is as if the dew of Hermon were falling on Mount Zion. For there the Lord bestows his blessing, even life forevermore."
(Psalm 133 NIV)

God loves unity. A marriage marked by unity or oneness is a place where each individual knows that they are fully loved and can flourish into their full potential. You are still uniquely you.

A marriage without oneness is lonely, painful, and empty. When we choose ourselves over our spouse, we reinforce their fear of being rejected. We leave them consistently asking the questions: Do you love me? Will you care for me? Do I matter?

Oneness is a selfless choice. Every day as a spouse, you get to set the tone for oneness. Not sameness. Oneness.

Oneness depends on you. Your level of marital satisfaction will be determined by your willingness to be one.

Oneness has no room for defensiveness.
Oneness is not selfish.
Oneness seeks to understand.
Oneness seeks the well-being of your partner.

In a state of oneness, our individuality gives. In separateness, our individuality takes.

Die to your differences, but not your dysfunction. You guys are different, we get it. But differences don't have to be the death of your relationship. As Christ followers, we are called to die to our differences and preferences so that we may grow in maturity. Learn what distinguishes a difference of preference or opinion from a true dysfunction. Any form of abuse is dysfunction. Whether the abuse is emotional, verbal, physical, or sexual, abuse is abuse. If dysfunctional behaviors exist in your marriage, seek help. Seek professional counsel. Above all, seek God.

"Those who belong to Christ Jesus have nailed the passions and desires of their sinful nature to his cross and crucified them there. Since we are living by the Spirit, let us follow the Spirit's leading in every part of our lives."
(Galatians 5:24-25 NLT)

Respond
How are you and your spouse different?

1. _____

2. _____

3._____

Oneness starts with taking responsibility for your individuality. It starts with committing that no matter what, you will bring your best self to your marriage.

You must make a commitment to yourself and your spouse to become one.

As a couple, one of the greatest ways to choose your spouse is to learn more about them. Getting to know each other deeply will create empathy, and empathy is an important step toward oneness.

We empathize with ourselves more than anyone else. We find it easy to hold other people to account for small mistakes and oversights, while excusing ourselves for the very same action.

Empathy creates unity.

An exercise in conversation:
Here are a few questions you can ask each other:

Q. Tell me about a difficult experience growing up.
Q. In kickball, were you first to be chosen or last? Or somewhere in between?
Q. What are your future dreams?
Q. How can I support your hopes?
Q. What can I do practically to calm your fears?

Oneness depends on you. Oneness depends on your using your individuality to complement your marriage, and to uniquely give

The above questions can be modified for any issue that is preventing oneness in your marriage.

1. Sex
2. Parenting
3. Spirituality and Relationship with God
4. Communication
5. Physical Health

It is impossible to discuss the totality of who you are about to marry before you tie the knot. The fullness of who your spouse is will be discovered over a lifetime. Disappointment can creep into a marriage when our expectations and reality do match. An important way to bring your individual expectations into alignment is to spend time dreaming together.

Dream Together:

1. Individually spend time writing a vision statement for the future. This should include plans, travel, family goals, and ventures.

2. Share your vision of your life together with your partner.

3. Observe the following questions:
   • What are the similarities?
   • What are the differences?
   • How can we integrate our dreams into one dream?

- What do we need to do to make these dreams a reality?
- What has to change?
- What commitment am I making today individually to move toward our shared goals?

Taking practical steps toward the future that you mutually envision will make each spouse feel heard and loved! Dreaming Together should happen on a regular basis, whether annually or monthly.

Remember, oneness in marriage is two people on one mission.

As you achieve and attain goals, the unity you experience as a couple will grow exponentially.

What do I need to surrender so that my spouse and I can become one on a greater level?

What do I wish my spouse understood about me?

IN A STATE OF ONENESS, OUR INDIVIDUALITY GIVES. IN SEPARATENESS, OUR INDIVIDUALITY TAKES.

Journal

Week Four

LISTENING + COMMUNICATION

Week Four
LISTENING + COMMUNICATION

Listening and communication are foundational to the success of any great marriage. These skills are not usually taught in school or in our homes. In fact, many of us have spent our lives observing poor communication and surface-level listening.

Today, distracted listening is practically acceptable, and yet harmful. Social media, devices of every kind pinging, Alexa waiting on our every request, and more, are seeking to garner your focus. In a world where anything and everything is vying for your attention, paying real attention to what your spouse is saying is a truly valuable gift.

Every person wants to be known and understood by their spouse. This is a major reason we get married—so that someone can know us, and we can know someone. Listening is critical to knowing and understanding another person and having the empathy necessary to care for them. When we truly listen to our spouse, we affirm them on the deepest level. When we do the difficult work of communicating, we create a pathway or channel of understanding.

Loving and respectful words and postures of heart are inherent in listening and communication. True listening and communication cannot be achieved through anger, control, or manipulation. One's guard must come down and the posture of the heart has to be one of surrender, respect, and love. It is possible you may have some behaviors that have to be unlearned, and some wounds that may need to heal.

Listening and communication create trust, trust creates openness, openness creates vulnerability. If respect and love are present, vulnerability leads to emotional need fulfillment, which builds trust. The more trust that is built, the more quickly we are able to arrive at vulnerability. The more vulnerability, the more intimacy. The more intimacy. . .well, you know. :)

Healthy communication creates a refuge for our spouse that cannot be found elsewhere.

When listening and communication work together, the flywheel of love, respect, joy, and intimacy begins to turn. The flywheel is an important metaphor. As these skills are practiced, the flywheel turns faster. As the flywheel turns, momentum is created. The more you listen and communicate on the small things and the big, the more you develop and store up trust. Trust is the kinetic energy of a strong and healthy marriage.

When you have genuine trust, communication becomes easier. Trust is the currency that helps you overcome the little issues. Sometimes poor communication is just the symptom, and lack of trust is the real problem. When trust is absent, the little issues become big fights, and the big and most necessary discussions are avoided because we are too busy making little molehills into major mountains.

Respond

TRUST

Ask yourself:

Do I trust my spouse?

_____

Do I trust myself?

_____

If I don't have trust, how can I develop trust, even incrementally?

_____

BARRIERS TO ENGAGEMENT

Listening

"Blessed is the man who listens to me, Watching daily at my gates, Waiting at the posts of my doors. For whoever finds me finds life, And obtains favor from the Lord." (Proverbs 8:34–35 NKJV)

The scripture above is about us listening to God's wisdom with anticipation.

The writer of the Proverbs encourages the reader to listen, watch, and wait, because afterward there is a reward. When we really listen to others, we give a gift, and we receive a gift. Listening and engagement is one of the most valuable blessings we can give, and when we truly dial in, the gift we receive is depth.

What keeps us from giving our best to our spouse? What are your barriers to engagement?

Social Media
It can be easy to tune out our spouse with work, chores, kids, bills, Facebook, Instagram, Twitter, TikTok, and Snapchat demanding our attention? I mean, who has the time to listen intently to the one person we decided to commit our lives to—especially when we're learning the latest dance?

What if your consumption of social media makes listening to real people feel like overload?

Our brains were only designed to take in so much information. Perhaps we have over-prioritized what is least important and under-prioritized what is most important.

Next to God, your relationship with your spouse is most important. Being aware of their needs, their schedule, their struggles, and their joy is critical to the health and quality of your relationship.

We are in control of our time and the attention we give. Social media can be prioritized, and does not have to be eliminated altogether, but it should rank among the lowest of the low—with our spouse among the top.

Familiarity
The age-old problem. Familiarity. We get so familiar with our husband or wife that we stop valuing them as highly as they deserve. It's just them. We give our kids our best attention, our work, social media, friends, other positive obligations like volunteering or church. So often our spouse gets the leftovers.

Or worse, through conflict and unresolved issues, we discount and diminish what they have to say and intentionally tune them out. Worse, we get defensive, combative, or critical whenever they offer something.

Have you stopped listening to your spouse? Or do you possibly feel unheard?

Perhaps you're in a cycle of ignoring and being ignored. If so, the best thing I can say to you is that today you can choose to break the cycle to reveal healthy and loving communication.

Thankfully, every person in every marriage can learn the art and science of Communication and Listening. Some people are natural communicators and listeners, and others are not. These are skills that can be acquired, developed, practiced, and implemented. The more skilled you become, the more trust you can build.

COMMUNICATION

"Let not mercy and truth forsake you; Bind them around your neck, Write them on the tablet of your heart, And so find favor and high esteem in the sight of God and man." (Proverbs 3:3–4 NKJV)

This scripture provides the ingredients for godly communication and tells you exactly how it will turn out if you listen and follow the instructions.

The results for employing mercy and truth? Favor and high esteem in the sight of God and people.

Mercy and Truth

Mercy and Truth are peers, equally necessary to healthy communication. Neither is less, and neither is more. Each personality is unique, and our style of communication is connected to our personality. However, the scriptures exist to transform us, never to validate who we already are.

If you are harsh, cultivate mercy.
If you are weak in being honest about your feelings, cultivate truth.

God's style of communication always begins with mercy. Mercy looks like kindness and gentleness, encouragement, and affirmation. When someone encourages me individually and specifically, it is miraculous. All distraction melts away, and focus becomes my superpower. You too? I thought it was just me.
Conversely, when someone starts in on me with harsh and critical tones, I want to run to the ends of the earth. Funny how that works.

Marriage communication is no different. We don't get a pass on grace and mercy because we're married. In fact, it should the place we bring our best encouragement and all our self-control. Too often, our spouse is the dumping ground for our stress, pain, and chaos, and somehow, we think it's ok.

Listening + Encouragement

At that time a severe famine struck the land of Canaan, forcing Abram to go down to Egypt, where he lived as a foreigner. As he was approaching the border of Egypt, Abram said to his wife, Sarai, "Look, you are a very beautiful woman. When the Egyptians see you, they will say, 'This is his wife. Let's kill him; then we can have her!' So please tell them you are my sister. Then they will spare my life and treat me well because of their interest in you." (Genesis 12:10-13 NLT emphasis the author's)

Abram wants to tell a lie. He is in the process of relocating his family to Egypt and decides before they even get there that his wife is going to be taken and he is going to be killed. He has no basis for this and has received no threats. Yet his fear and concern are so real that they are driving him to do something stupid. Sarai went along with Abram's plan.

What if Sarai had encouraged Abram?
What if she had listened beyond the scheme and heard the fear?
What if she had a conversation that was honest and affirming?

It not likely that your husband or wife is actively convincing you to do something dishonest. But perhaps there is a lot that they are saying behind what they are actually saying. What if there is more emotion than we realize? Abram's fears were real. His promise from God was also real.

What if we are missing real opportunities to encourage our spouse's dreams and discourage their fears and insecurities? What if we could see those moments for what they really are?

You can choose the quality of your listening
You can choose the quality of your communication.
Just a few verses earlier, Abram had received a real, specific promise from God regarding his future. That was a fantastic opportunity for Sarai to remind Abram about what God had already said.

What if you were your spouse's biggest cheerleader? What if every time pain or fear or insecurity presented itself in our spouse, we were the ones to remind them of their strengths and their future?

And when things get tense, what if we led with kindness, encouragement, peace, and wisdom?

"She opens her mouth with wisdom, And on her tongue is the law of kindness." (Proverbs 31:26 NKJV)

We may not realize how powerful the voice of our spouse is in our lives. Their words carry more weight than perhaps anyone else's.

List one insecurity that your spouse has:

_____

Create a statement to encourage your spouse when that insecurity or fear pops up:

_____

TRUTH is…

Good communication will not allow mercy to stand alone. Truth is not second place to mercy. Rather, it is an equal part of the communication equation.

So often in our communication, we can leave mercy, encouragement, and kindness out altogether and go straight for the truth jugular, and we feel empowered to do so with our spouse. It's like we get deceived into thinking that our loud, critical, rude way will actually help get the point across and create a breakthrough of love, intimacy, and care.

Back to Abram and Sarai:

Listening + Truth

What if Sarai had combined encouragement with truth?
Something like:

"Abram, don't you remember? God said you would be the father of many nations, and I believe in you. I know that God has a future for us. I am so proud of who you are, and the man of integrity that you are. I am uncomfortable lying. I believe it devalues our belief in God's promise. I want to be on the same page with you, and I am committed to what we're doing, but I don't think we should move forward until we agree about how to proceed. Lying is not going to produce the result that we want. How else can we proceed?"

This is fictitious, of course, but this scenario could play out in any of our marriages.

Respond

How can I combine mercy and truth while communicating with my spouse?

_____

For the next five days:

Pray Proverbs 3:3 over yourself:

> **"Let not mercy and truth forsake you; Bind them around your neck, Write them on the tablet of your heart, And so find favor and high esteem in the sight of God and man."**
> **(Proverbs 3:3 NKJV)**

Dear God, I choose to be transformed by Proverbs 3:3. I am a person of mercy and truth, and that balance will be expressed in my life. I bind them around my neck, I write them on the tablet of my heart, and I will find favor and high esteem in Your sight and my spouse's sight. Amen.

I have been praying this scripture for years, and as imperfect as I am, I have grown significantly. I am less reactive, calmer, and I try to be respectful first.

I want you to know:

1. I did not force a behavior change and become someone I am not.
2. This had nothing to do with my personality or innate communication style.
3. The Word of God transformed me, the real me, into a healthier, more loving, and God-honoring version of me.
4. I like this me better, and so do other people.

Exercise:
These phrases will let your spouse know you need to talk about more than just dinner:
1. "This is important to me."
2. "I need you to hear me right now."
3. "Can we talk at a time when there are no distractions?"

Create opportunities for communication and listening to take place:

1. Set the tone for great conversations
2. Find the right time and place free from technology, kids, and other distractions
3. Validate and encourage who your spouse is
4. Use "I" statements, not "You" for example: "I would like to. . ."

Frequency Matters

Let's face it: Our emotional love tank runs dry, and one of the best ways to maintain healthy levels for each partner is to check in regularly. Set a time on a weekly or consistent basis to connect as a couple. Conversation should be more than the latest school functions, bills, and decisions. It should be about inquiring after your spouse's heart. Choose a few or all of these questions to ask each other. If you are not used to this style of communication, pick the one you feel is most benign and ask each other that one question consistently.

Weekly Marriage Check In:

1. Is there anything I can do for you in this moment to help you feel more comfortable or loved?

2. How can I better support you in your life?

3. Do you think you will need more closeness or more alone time over the next couple of days?

4. Is there any argument that we had this past week that you feel incomplete about?

5. What are the main stressors currently in your life, and is there any way I can alleviate that stress for you, if only a small amount?

6. Is there anything I have done in the past week that may have unknowingly hurt you?

7. How can I pray for you or with you?

8. How can I meet your sexual needs and desires? How would you like to be pursued?

" **HEALTHY COMMUNICATION CREATES A REFUGE FOR OUR SPOUSE THAT CANNOT BE FOUND ELSEWHERE.**

Journal

Week Five

CONFLICT AND RESOLUTION

Week Five

CONFLICT AND RESOLUTION

There is something you should know: EVERY MARRIAGE HAS CONFLICT.

Excuse me for shouting. It's rude, I know.

Every. Single. Marriage. Has. Conflict. Us included.

My husband and I see and do things very differently, and you can probably relate. As I shared in "Our Story," he is steady, strong, incredibly smart, and the impulse section at Target has no power over him. He is a saver, but also a risk taker—after calculated due diligence, of course. I am also smart, strong, and a risk taker, but I don't know that I would always have been described as steady. I can get really excited about strategic ideas that have no basis in reality, and even begin to take action before any appropriate research has taken place. I can be excitable and spontaneous—focused on the immediate. In short, the impulse section at Target still holds sway over me. Please tell me, who doesn't need more Chapstick in their life?

In my less mature days, I used to believe that his different approach to life and decision-making was something I needed to change. I wanted him to make decisions more quickly and be excited with me. I could easily create conflict about our difference in style rather than the issue at hand.

As I grew more mature, I began to see the genius in his style. We made less mistakes, and things turned out better in the long-term. I learned that patience is power. I've stopped trying to change him. I respect and admire his style and have tried to adopt it as my own.

Don't worry, I bring strengths to our relationship too. I just think you might learn more from my hard-won lessons than you ever will from my pretending I've always had it altogether.

Conflict just is. People have opposing viewpoints, they disagree, they disappoint, they fail to meet expectations and needs, they overpromise, and sometimes, they betray.

Every marriage is as unique as the individuals within. There is no way to compare the conflict within your marriage with someone else's. Conflict will vary in type, style, and amount. So, stop comparing. Your background is complex and deserves the appropriate amount of space without the pressure of comparison.

Conflict is complicated, and a thriving marriage is no accident. Intentionally addressing the topics of conflict and applying tools that lead us toward agreement will help us enjoy marriage more deeply. When conflict is thoroughly resolved, our hearts are clean, and we are free from anger and frustration to live out our best lives. So, let's address the main points of conflict—the sore spots—and discover how to dig under the conflict and criticism to find resolution in our marriage and respect for each other.

Marital conflict is unlike any other disagreement or misunderstanding we experience in life. In friendships, business partnerships, and other relationships, you are free to walk away when conflict gets too complicated. In marriage, it's not that simple. You're one. You made a commitment to stay together in the face of conflict, adversity, negativity, and more.

Let's study the scripture and sharpen our tools. Society values those who can win arguments, but God celebrates the one who seeks resolution.

Scriptures to pray:

"Blessed are the peacemakers, For they will be called sons of God."
(Matthew 5:9 NKJV)

"Avoiding a fight is a mark of honor; only fools insist on quarreling."
(Proverbs 20:3 NLT)

"He who is slow to anger is better than the mighty, he who rules his spirit than he who takes a city."
(Proverbs 16:32 NKJV)

"The discretion of a man makes him slow to anger, And his glory is to overlook a transgression." (Proverbs 19:11 NKJV)

In the right setting, with the right heart, at the right time, there is no conflict that cannot be resolved.

We should desire resolution, unity, and mutually satisfying outcomes. Being right, winning, or getting our way may offer short-term bragging rights, but ultimately will erode trust, then steal intimacy that is necessary to build a strong and lasting union.

One of marriage's greatest attributes is being safe. When conflict remains open and unresolved there is no potential to thrive. Our brains are wired to seek resolution, and our hearts need to know that all is well. Marriage feels safe when we have openly and honestly said what we needed to, felt heard and understood, and know deeply that our well-being is valued by another.

God Himself goes to great lengths to communicate that He has forgiven us of sin. The spiritual conflict between He and us has been resolved and we are free to thrive.

Have you given your spouse that same gift?

Respond

Our top 3 issues of conflict include:

1. _____

2. _____

3. _____

Take some time to discuss what you both wrote down. Do not let this escalate into a conflict about conflict.

These conflicts are valid and exist for important reasons. Mutual awareness is the first step. The next level stuff happens when you decide as a couple that you are going to address the conflicts in a consistently healthy way.

By making this decision, you are setting the stage for a marriage rich with intimacy, both emotional and physical. This is partnership. Resolving conflict in healthy and respectful ways is when and where real trust is built.

Four Conflict Classrooms

As a child, how did you observe conflicts being handled and resolved—or perhaps left unresolved? How you grew up was like a classroom, where you learned relationship skills for the most formative eighteen or so years of your life. Have you carried any of the conflict classrooms into your marriage?

Below you'll find just four styles of conflict. This is not exhaustive, but a simple overview of our conflict patterns. Each one of us may identify with one or all these styles.

1. **The Avoider** - The avoider is seeking peace but is only able to obtain a false and temporary sense of it. When we avoid issues and conflicts that need resolution, we are really just packing them away for a later day. All our hope that they will magically disappear only serves to multiply and intensify our problems. Avoidance, if allowed, creates a lack of safety within the relationship, because no one is ever sure if we're actually ok. On the surface, all may seem well. But underneath, our unresolved problems are brewing and stewing.

Thoughts for the avoider:
1. Fear: Why are you afraid to fully address conflict with your spouse? What are you afraid may happen as a result if you discuss problems thoroughly?
2. Where did you first observe people avoiding conflict?
3. How can you take baby steps to open up to your spouse?
4. How can your spouse support you?

Scripture for Avoidance Style:

"For God has not given us a spirit of fear, but of power, love and of a sound mind." (2 Timothy 1:7 NKJV)

Pray This:
God, please help me get past the fear of conflict with my spouse and heal from any past experiences that may be affecting my present. Help me to love my spouse deeply and walk in the intimacy and care that you created for marriage. Amen.

2.**The Grudge Holder** – The Grudge Holder is always keeping score. Often when an argument arises, the Grudge Holder dredges up some relic of the past to prove their point. They feel justified spouting off a litany of offenses they've had to endure and reminding the other spouse of just how much they have had to put up with. They can be harsh and hurtful. The Grudge Holder has not truly forgiven and is usually hurting deeply themselves. They typically carry both pain and pride, and the spouse on the other side of the Grudge Holder has difficulty knowing which one to address. Sometimes the Grudge Holder has expectations that are too high and have not been communicated. Recognizing that your spouse is just a human can help.

Thoughts for the Grudge Holder:

1. See past the pain and see the person. Your spouse is imperfect, just like you.

2. Discover why you have difficulty releasing offense and pain. Discuss with your spouse.

3. What small steps can you take to bring true closure to offenses and healing in your marriage?

4. Invite God to heal the pain and help you address the pride. Study Scripture on these topics.

Scripture for the Grudge Holder:

"Therefore, as God's chosen people, holy and dearly loved, clothe yourselves with compassion, kindness, humility, gentleness and patience. Bear with each other and forgive one another if any of you has a grievance against someone. Forgive as the Lord forgave you. And over all these virtues put on love, which binds them all together in perfect unity." (Colossians 3:12–13 NIV)

"Heal me, O Lord, and I shall be healed; Save me, and I shall be saved, For You are my praise."
(Jeremiah 17:14 NKJV)

Pray This:
God, I surrender all of the pain and all of the past to Your wise and loving hands. I trust that You know exactly what to do. Please heal me of the wounds that are still festering

and help me gain a deep sense of your forgiveness—that I may freely and fully forgive my spouse and those in my life. Amen.

3. **The Competitor** - "I know, I know, I know." These are often the words of those who follow this conflict pattern. The Competitor knows it all, has done it all, did it better than anyone else, or knows someone who did. The Competitor vacillates between the defense or offense depending on what it might take to win the argument. Winning is everything, and appearing to be right at all costs is downright expensive. The Competitor has deep insecurities that never allow their spouse to have the perceived upper hand. They have yet to realize that the real beauty in marriage is mutuality which stems from individual humility, and that being wrong or apologizing is never about weakness— and always about strength. A competitive nature is not wrong. But competition has a context, and marriage ain't it. Your spouse is your teammate, not your challenger.

Marriage is safety and service, not winning and losing.

Thoughts for the Competitor:

1. How do you compete with your spouse? Do you regularly argue a point beyond reasonable boundaries?

2. Train yourself to recognize when you're competing for competition's sake.

3. Choose to approach conflict with humility, empathy, and solutions.

4. Allow your spouse to remind you when your competitive nature is finding its way into the wrong context.

Scripture for the Competitor:

"For you have been called to live in freedom, my brothers and sisters. But don't use your freedom to satisfy your sinful nature. Instead, use your freedom to serve one another in love." (Galatians 5:13 NLT)

"But what things were gain to me, these I have counted loss for Christ." (Philippians 3:7 NKJV)

Pray this:

God, I surrender my nature, my personality, and my desire to be right to You. Give me a heart that listens to You first, then my spouse. Help me to be there for my spouse and to put their needs and viewpoints above my own. It is my desire to seek unity and togetherness. Help me to do so. Amen.

4. **The Collaborator** - You collab instead of reacting. Bingo! This is healthy communication. This does not mean that conflict does not arise, au contraire—conflict exists in every marriage. The collaborator is always trying to seek the highest good and mutual resolution. Seeking the highest good will always result in the betterment of the union, not just a person. It takes empathy and maturity to work in a collaborative way with your spouse. While difficult, it is possible. You can train yourself to collaborate with them instead of reacting to them.

In music, we love collabs because they bring out the best of two unique artists to create one incredible song. They are different artists with specific styles, but that specificity never diminishes their individual strengths. In fact, it makes for mind-blowing music when two artistic geniuses are brought together. I think we also love artists who collaborate because we often see them as competitors. We love to see them lay down the competition and unite.

Marriage is similar. Let's face it, you're both amazing. Marriage is richer and more beautiful when we respect each other's strengths. We often focus too much time on the other person's deficiencies and not enough time on finding ways to collaborate.

Thoughts for the Collaborator:

1. When conflict arises, how can I serve my spouse in greater ways?

2. If my spouse does not reciprocate in collaboration, how can I communicate my heart for cooperation in the middle of conflict?

3. What are my personal areas of growth that will benefit my marriage?

Scripture for the Collaborator:

Love is patient, love is kind. It does not envy, it does not boast, it is not proud. It does not dishonor others, it is not self-seeking, it is not easily angered, it keeps no record of wrongs. Love does not delight in evil but rejoices with the truth. It always protects, always trusts, always hopes, always perseveres. Love never fails. . . (1 Corinthians 13:4-8 NIV)

Prayer for the Collaborator:
God, thank you for the wisdom to cooperate in conflict. I pray my marriage continues to strengthen as we serve and submit to one another. For the areas that may be harder to collaborate, I pray you give us what we need to walk through them with grace for each other and peace that only comes from You. Amen.

Respond

My spouse's top 3 strengths in our relationship:

1.
2.
3.

Now take a moment and share with your spouse how you see their areas of strength. Consistently encourage your spouse regarding their unique strengths and train yourself to rely on their strengths in the middle of conflict.

Practical Tools

Seek To Understand

Raise your hand if you have ever fought with your spouse for a prolonged period of time and made no progress toward reasonable resolution. Us too. A large obstacle in the path of the conflict resolution we seek is hyper self-focus. We defend our positions and dredge up old arguments. We are stymied because we are stubborn. On the marital battlefield, I forget that my spouse is not my sworn enemy.

As that slowly dawns on me, I drop my emotional weapons of war and call for a truce. Resolution, healing, unity, and intimacy continue.

So, what actually happens between launching a nuclear attack and waving the white flag?

My personal experience involves an about-face. That neatly fits into my military analogy, but also means a reversal of attitude or behavior.

This about-face is a strategic advantage in conflict. It is moving from defending to understanding.

Take a moment to think about the people you respect. We generally have respect for people who have invested into our lives—people like mentors, teachers, parents, and pastors. Because of our respect for them, we bring a sense of genuine openness to every conversation. If they have a piece of wisdom for us or point out an area where we need to grow, many times we're grateful that they care so much.

Now. . .
Your spouse wants to bring up an area of growth, or some issue has erupted into a full-on war.
Do you respect them enough to bring that same genuine sense of openness to what they will say?

Will you seek to understand where they are coming from?

Will you have the same gratitude?

Or will you defend, shut down, and try to control?

When you seek to understand, rather than defend, fight, and shut down, you save yourself hours of unnecessary fighting. You keep at bay the temptation to say hurtful words that last far beyond the moment. You preserve your emotional energy for the positive, rather than wasting it away on the negative.

What if we started every conflict with respect and resolution in mind?

Practice A Soft Answer

"A soft answer turns away wrath, but a harsh word stirs up anger."
(Proverbs 15:1 NKJV)

Love your spouse enough to change your posture, tone of voice, facial expression, and body language. The scripture above is giving a path toward the calm that we seek. Like anything else, you can train yourself and be transformed by God's word to build unity and love.

I feel that the number one issue we fight about is: _____

Describe your personal harsh reaction: _____

What can you do differently to bring a soft answer?: _____

Do Not Go to Bed Angry

This may seem incredibly outdated, like something Grandma and Grandpa used to say. Grandma and Grandpa were probably married mostly happily for fifty to seventy years.

Ben and I have personally practiced this for over twenty years. I have known couples who allow themselves to go to bed angry. Once they have done so, they speak of a growing chasm of emotional distance in their relationship that shows up by morning. An increasing dislike for their spouse. A desire to be away from them as often as possible.

I have never once heard someone share how going to bed angry with their spouse created resolution, intimacy, forgiveness, and closeness.

If you feel this is an outdated maxim, you're right. It's really old.

It's found in the pages of Scripture:

"Be angry, and do not sin": do not let the sun go down on your wrath."
(Ephesians 4:26 NKJV)

The real issue with "going to bed angry" is that we are not focused on resolution but holding onto to the offense. God desires that we are quick to forgive and seek loving and mutual resolution in our marriage.

In the words of Elsa: "Let it go." Get a good night's sleep knowing that you're growing closer to your spouse and not further apart. If the issue is deeper, seek wise counsel or actual counseling to address hurts, trauma, and other issues preventing you both from forward motion.

Take a moment to make a commitment to God, yourself, and your spouse that when conflict arises, going to bed angry or unresolved is no longer an option.

Forgive

Every conflict should end with stated forgiveness. This creates a strong sense of "where we are," as in: "Are we good?" It creates a communication habit and provides opportunity to state our care for each other.

When it comes to forgiveness, don't follow your feelings. Choices lead, feelings follow.

Forgiveness Habit:
The below exercise can be useful for the spouse who started the argument or perhaps for both spouses to say to each other. It's been my experience that in most cases, we're both at fault in some way.

I am sorry for _____
Will you please forgive me?
Yes, I forgive you
I want to help you / meet your need / understand your viewpoint
Have we resolved the conflict? Or are we reconciled?
I love you and I am committed to you.

" **IN THE RIGHT SETTING, WITH THE RIGHT HEART, AT THE RIGHT TIME, THERE IS NO CONFLICT THAT CANNOT BE RESOLVED.**

Journal

Week Six

CHOOSING SAFEGUARDS FOR YOUR MARRIAGE

CHOOSING SAFEGUARDS FOR YOUR MARRIAGE

Safeguard: a measure taken to protect someone or something or to prevent something undesirable.

I love all of the wedding language we use in our culture.

You said "yes" and immediately posted your engagement photo and finalized your wedding day hashtag to collect all of the Insta-worthy moments on the countdown to the big day. Next, you said "yes to the dress," and commemorated it with photos and girlfriends. Then there were the pre-wedding social gatherings, the monogrammed bridesmaid gifts, choreographing the groomsmen dance, the seating chart, the photographer and videographer, and deciding upon first look pics with hubby. Then it's finally the wedding day, filled with emotion and wonder—a day you will not soon forget. You've danced your last dance, you dash through the sparkler tunnel, hoping not to singe your hair and then you jet off to Fiji for your honeymoon, return home to open gifts, send thank you notes, and watch your wedding video four thousand times.

Or some version of that.

After the hustle and the bustle is over, you settle into married life, which is the very reason for all that activity, planning, and that one giant special day.

And then your spouse does something irritating—painfully, excruciatingly, offensively irritating—and your first married fight ensues.

Or some version of that.

All the preparation and planning for the day did not prepare you for the thousands of days that would follow. Hard days, special days, painful days, boring days, great days, beautiful days, lonely days, complex days, and all the other days.

Our wedding day is filled with plans, maybe even some backup plans, and quite possibly in a world like ours, some backup plans to the backup plans.

But what of our plans to enrich and safeguard the union we so meticulously planned to celebrate? Did we make plans to grow as an individual? Have we discussed how we're

Oxford Languages. "Safeguard." Google's English Dictionary.

going to mature as a couple? Have we mapped out the lines that we plan not to cross? Or perhaps even articulated them within our own hearts?

This week is designed to help you define and choose safeguards for your marriage so that you know where some important lines are. The lines I speak of are, unfortunately, invisible to the physical eye most often.

Many times, the lines that we cross or boundaries that we violate are inside first. We can often think no one sees, but God always does.

"For the Lord does not see as man sees; for man looks at the outward appearance, but the Lord looks at the heart."

(1 Samuel 16:7 NKJV)

X-Ray Vision

God has it and we don't. He can see the deepest parts of our hearts, right down to our motives, fears, complaints, and hopes. While we can't see our own heart, we do live inside our own head. Between us and God, we are the only ones who really know what is happening in there. Because God sees us at our core, we can trust that if we surrender our marriages and our actions to Him, He will guide us where we need to go.

No one got started on their married life with the expectation or intentional desire to fail. And yet, we all know people or perhaps have personally experienced failure. That failure could range from consistent poor treatment of their spouse all the way to divorce court. No matter what you've experienced in matrimony, be encouraged. It can be better. And when we know better, we can choose better.

God gives us safeguards that can help prevent the pain we pray to avoid. We have a part to play in the health, quality, and enjoyment of marriages. Safeguarding today brings peace tomorrow.

Commitment:

I choose to do my part to safeguard my marriage by safeguarding my own heart.

Thoughts

Thoughts are the building blocks for our actions. Science tells us that our thoughts are real things that have real impact on our brain, our behavior, and our lives. As usual, scripture confirms science and science confirms scripture.
We often think the greatest threat to our marriage is external to us, but perhaps the first enemy is within. Our thoughts have tremendous power over the quality of our lives and sinful or negative thoughts consistently repeated will bring about negative consequences.

"For as he thinks in his heart, so is he. . ." (Proverbs 23:7 NKJV)

Our brains are like sponges, waiting for data to be downloaded. Once it is, our thoughts process said data, which then, in turn, affects our mood, our behavior, our habits, and the course of our lives.

This world wants to download its beliefs, ideas, and values around family and marriage. Of course, so does God. We have to remain cognizant and vigilant of which voice we are listening to and what we are thinking about. For every thought we think, it's easy to think it again and again, until we become what we are thinking about.

Respond

Do my thoughts surrounding my marriage and my spouse please God?

_____

_____

Did you know that you have control over your thoughts? The frustrated ones, the negative ones, even the daydreaming ones, that take you to a different life entirely? You can create a positive thought pattern for your spouse and your marriage.
You can choose to focus on the good, appreciate what's right, and stop dwelling on everything you wish would change.

We demolish arguments and every pretension that sets itself up against the knowledge of God, and we take captive every thought to make it obedient to Christ. And we will be ready to punish every act of disobedience, once your obedience is complete. (2 Corinthians 10:5–6 NIV)

At the end of this week's content, I share my personal thought pattern for my marriage and provide space for you to create one of your own.

Steps to Safeguard

What I Take in
"Blessed are the pure in heart, For they shall see God." (Matthew 5:8 NKJV)

What do you read? What are you binging on Netflix? And what are taking in through social media? Everything we take in shapes our brain, our hearts, and our values. Imagine that your heart is like a lump of clay. Everything you see, hear, and focus on is constantly shaping that clay for better or worse, forming and informing what you do and who you are. What do you ultimately want to look like?

Societal Viewpoints
Have you ever noticed that shows and movies tend to negatively portray a long-term marriage commitment and glorify attraction, sex, and romance? I can think of very few shows on cable or streaming services that depict a married couple making their way through the landmines of life in a truly positive way. If it's a comedy, one spouse is the butt of every joke and generally demoralized. Or perhaps it's a drama where a spouse is betrayed. There are very few entertainment resources that truly celebrate a long-term, respectful, loving marital union. Being aware of this can help safeguard your marriage through appropriate limits.

Conversation with Friends or Family
Conversations with friends can either be rich sources of encouragement or venting sessions that don't really help.

Beware the friend that always wants to talk negatively about his or her spouse. If you don't reciprocate with a few negatives from time to time, it's likely they'll start asking: "Doesn't your spouse ever do that?" or "Why does your marriage seem so perfect?" It may seem like they are asking for advice—just a negative example, perhaps. Don't take the bait. There is a massive difference between discussing solutions and gossiping about ongoing problems. When your friend starts the bashing, you can start encouraging and directing them toward resources that can help. There is a fine line between empathizing and affirming. While their difficulties are valid and real, it is ok to recognize you're not equipped to solve them. But point them to places or people that can.

Social Media

Have you ever been envious of the adorable couples doing perfectly synchronized TikTok dances? Have you ever thought to yourself, "Why isn't that us?" Keep in mind, those "couples" may just be a couple of friends who have practiced a gazillion times, and they are trying to get a billion followers on the IG. Any married couple you observe on any social platform is showing you a mere fifteen seconds to a minute of their lives. It's not real. I repeat, it is not real. Why? Because it is not the full picture. It's not the good, the bad, and the ugly. It's only the good. We have to monitor how much social media we are consuming because it shapes what we believe. We get indoctrinated with the belief that everyone is doing better than we are at having more fun and living their best married lives. When we begin to believe that people on social media live better lives than us, we are holding our marriages to unfair standards and that will create frustration and disappointment. Your spouse deserves better.

Pornography (of any sort)

Movies, books, pictures etc.

Pornography, even in the marriage context, is never ok. It illustrates a false reality that can never be achieved and distorts the purity and intimacy God intended for marriage. There is a multitude of research, both Christian and non-Christian, that speaks to the destructive nature of porn. It may create a fleeting feeling, but it destroys real intimacy with one person.

Respond

Is there anything I need to stop taking in, watching, or listening to?

_____

Have I adopted the world's view of marriage or God's view?

_____

Comparison

Comparison is a killer—a subtle assassin. Comparing your spouse with someone else's will only negatively impact your thoughts and feelings about who your spouse is and who they are becoming. There is a massive difference between comparisons and examples. Examples are not comparisons. Comparisons are not examples.

How can you know the difference? Comparisons are competitive and examples show you the way. If you just want what they have, but they can't show you the way, you're comparing. If there is no pressure to compete because they are so much further down the road than you, they are an example, and you can learn a lot from them. Find couples that have been imperfectly but successfully married for ten, twenty, or thirty more years than you. Without comparison, allow them to show you the way.

Do I competitively compare my marriage or feel inferior to others?

Yes or No

_____

Wise Counsel and Counseling

Every marriage needs positive influences. We all need examples we can look to that help illustrate standards and safeguards that make a marriage strong, healthy, and safe. We need to seek wise counsel in the scripture, books, podcasts, and, of course, mentors.

Sometimes, that is just not enough, however. We may need to move beyond counsel and into counseling. There is absolutely no shame in this, and it may be exactly what you need to overcome major hurdles in your marriage.

Who is my wise counsel? (People)

_____

Where do I receive wise counsel? (Books, podcasts, other resources)

_____

Steps to Identify a Counselor
1. Pray and ask God to lead you
2. Determine what you are seeking to achieve
   (Communication Breakthrough, Healing, Building Trust after Betrayal)
3. Discuss with your spouse
4. Ask for referrals from trusted sources, or start searching online
5. Develop a list of questions that are important to you to interview a potential counselor

a. Are you married?
b. Have you ever been divorced?
c. Do you have children?
d. Are you a Christian? Where do you attend church?
e. What resources do you recommend?
f. Do you pray with couples?

Can I encourage you to create an intentional and godly thought pattern for your marriage that you will carry with you throughout married life?

Here is mine:

"I will serve my husband faithfully, spirit, soul, and body all the days of my life."

I have repeated this to myself thousands of times over the course of twenty years of marriage and plan to repeat thousands more. It has become me. When my brain wants to drift into negative thought patterns, complaining thoughts, drifting thoughts, or the enemy wants to bring thoughts of temptation, this is my touchstone.

It is a simple statement and has become a safeguard and refuge from the negativity that exists all around us.

Let's create yours:

1. What is the greatest influence on my thoughts?

_____

_____

_____

2. How can I safeguard my influences?

_____

_____

_____

3. Where can I find wise counsel?

_____

_____

_____

"I CHOOSE TO DO MY PART TO SAFEGUARD MY MARRIAGE BY SAFEGUARDING MY OWN HEART.

Journal

Week Seven

CHOOSING INTIMACY

Week Seven
CHOOSING INTIMACY

Your love delights me,
   my treasure, my bride.
Your love is better than wine,
   your perfume more fragrant than spices.
(Song of Solomon 4:10 NLT)

Let's talk about sex

Your sex life belongs in your prayer life. What? You've never heard that before? Me neither, until I started trying it and it made a difference in the quality of intimacy in my sex life.

Growing up as a Christian, I was never taught much about sex and intimacy. I mostly heard, "Don't do it until you're married." or "If you do it, you'll get pregnant and ruin your life." That was couched in much negative connotation and glowering facial expressions. I was left with the impression that sex was bad until it was permitted. No one ever told me it was supposed to be good—and was a powerful key to a whole and healthy marriage.

To boot, I certainly never heard that sex in the context of marriage was always intended by God to be physical, emotional, and spiritual. That limited communication created a mystery—a vacuum that left the world, my assumptions, perceptions, movies, friends, and negative experiences to find out what it really is. And then I got married, and suddenly it was sanctioned and even sacred. This made for a very incomplete idea of it. So, I had the bits I had pieced together, plus trying to be a godly Christian wife, all into one paradigm. My competing internal narratives left me confused, and in some ways, ashamed of it. I knew I was supposed to do it in the context of marriage, but no one ever said I was supposed to like it. I tried to be brave and pretend I understood it all, when underneath it all, I was a mess.

For the love, can we stop calling sex "it"? That alone will be an important step forward.

My hope is to help the girls growing up behind me to have a healthy, God-defined view of sex and intimacy. I pray that the younger generation will never have to wonder, question, or source the deets from the wrong places. Here are a few thoughts:

PSA #1: God is the author of sex—the actual physical act and all of its beauty and passion. He created you with the hormones, the drive, the equipment, and desire.

PSA #2: God created sex for pleasure, and He wants you to enjoy it completely.

PSA #3: Sex is an expression of intimacy, and intimacy is never just about sex and physical release alone. It is about your souls, your service to one another, and the choices you make to love yourself and your spouse completely.

No matter your view of sex or how it has impacted you up to this point, this week is about understanding God's original design for marital intimacy and integrating your spirituality with your sexuality. His design is far more fulfilling than having married, tired sex occasionally. True intimacy can add a whole new dimension of satisfaction to your marriage and personal effectiveness in your life.

This week's content will not provide everything you need to know about sex, or what is permissible and what's not. I will recommend some fantastic resources for this. This week is instead about choosing God-intended sexual intimacy, reprogramming your beliefs, and creating a foundation of relational intimacy for good sex to be built upon.

Choosing intimacy is about making the decision to develop and nurture the sexual side of your marriage relationship. This could mean talking about it with your spouse, praying about it, counseling, trying some new things that are agreed upon, or prioritizing sex and intimacy. It could also mean choosing to be a more giving partner before or during sex.

What can you choose today?

You can choose to not allow the world to inform your sexual identity or your values.
You can choose to invite God into your intimate life.
You can choose to initiate sex and intimacy more frequently to meet your spouse's needs and your own needs.
You can choose to put more effort into each time you and your spouse are together.

A turning point came when I began to pray before sex. Just a short, simple prayer by myself led to more enjoyment of sex because I finally began to understand that God wasn't against it. He is actually for it because (surprise), He designed it. That led to reading books and blogs by Christian authors on the topic of sex and learning more about the spiritual foundation and what is encouraged in sex. All of that led to an entirely undiscovered part of myself and a layer of beauty in my marriage that I never thought possible.

This week I will share my exact prayer with you, the books that I read, and some of the lessons I have personally discovered. My hope is that you find your own place of undiscovered beauty that is waiting for the two of you.

Choosing God-intended Intimacy

Sexual intimacy was designed by God for physical pleasure and to create a deep bond of physical and emotional trust. True sexual intimacy is an expression of unity, love, and trust. It has the power to heal and to propel us to be our best selves. God takes our deepest need for love and our physical desire for sex and produces intimacy. True intimacy produces wholeness.

God's intention for physical intimacy to be shared with one person speaks to the power inherent in the sexual relationship. We are to steward our sexuality responsibly. The sexual experience impacts our souls like nothing else, because there never has been and never will be anything casual about sex.

Sex is so powerful that Satan has tried to convince the world it was his idea and that everything sexy—and real sexual pleasure—is found apart from God. He wants you to believe that God has a low view of sex, and that He averts His eyes every time you do the deed. The reality is, sex is and was God's idea. His desire is that your relationship be filled with mutually satisfying physical intimacy where both partners are safe, secure, and whole. God wants you to have the best of it all: intense sexual pleasure, passion, attraction, desire, fulfillment, and an incredibly loving, trusting, and committed relationship. There, you and your spouse's emotional needs are met, your physical needs are met, and you carry a deep sense of belonging that breeds confidence and security. This picture of marriage is possible. It will never be perfect. It will never be every single thing you need at the moment you need it. But it will breed the deep bond of intimacy and love that you are seeking. Healthy expressions of sexual intimacy are the pinnacle of a thriving marriage.

Sex, in the worldly sense, is about pushing the physical boundaries and continual exploration to achieve physical satisfaction. But guess what? It's never enough. Sex without love will always lack something. In intimacy with our marriage partner, we find something deeply satisfying that transcends an orgasm or a fleeting sexual encounter. Sex plus intimacy bonds us together and then reinforces that bond. The strength of the bond is first for us as partners, and then it reaches into every aspect of our lives. This strong and loving bond also flows to our children, and they live in a deep security knowing that there is an unspoken wholeness in their parents. The thriving marriage has the potential to create thriving children and a whole family has the power to positively impact the world around them.

People often use sex to scratch the itch for love. But as many of us painfully know, love is not required for sex, and sex is not required for love. Sex alone cannot and will not fulfill your deepest needs, and a sexless marriage will be incomplete even if love is present.

Sex alone will never satisfy your soul. It wasn't designed that way. Sex is the just the surface level. Intimacy touches our deepest need for belonging. Sex was created to exist in the context of a monogamous, loving, healthy marital union.

The Song of Solomon is a beautiful example and expression of God's intention for sex and sexuality. He prioritizes the intimate relationship between a husband and wife so much that He dedicated an entire book of the Bible to the subject. This book is abstract with metaphors and language used in ancient times. It hardly feels relatable. While the Song of Solomon is a bit difficult to understand, studying it will help you know how important true marital intimacy and physical pleasure is to God.

Did you know the Bible is the only religious text of all world religions that devotes an entire book to sexuality and sensuality?

Respond

Try reading Song of Solomon Chapter 1 together.

How can you make choices leading toward deeper intimacy with your spouse?

1. Physically?
2. Emotionally?
3. Spiritually?

Reprogramming your Beliefs

Every person reading this book has a different sexual history. Some of us know the pain and trauma of abuse or violation. Some of us have made decisions that we're not proud of. Some of us have hurt others, and some have been hurt.

Since sex is a part of our God-given human nature, that means it has always been with us—from the first time we felt arousal until today. And many of us carry beliefs that distort God's best for sexual intimacy. God's desire is that you are healed from any negativity that robs from the beauty He intends.

Here is just a sample of some of the lies we believe:

Lie #1: "Women don't or shouldn't enjoy sex as much as men"
Women may enjoy it differently, and all women may not have the drive men do, but that does not disqualify women from desiring and enjoying sex with their husband. This lie will undermine your relationship and take away the intimate dimension designed for marriage.

"Sex is not an audition for dating. It's a privilege for the married." -Unknown

It's a privilege, not a chore, and the quality of your intimate life does not have to begin with abundant desire. You are encouraged by God to desire, pursue, and enjoy sex, sexiness, and intimacy with your spouse. Did you even read the Song of Solomon? Hello. You can choose to develop and nurture your sex life before the desire is present, or because the desire is present. In either case, ditch the lie and choose to foster more intimacy and better sex in your relationship.

Lie #2: "It should be perfect and natural every time"
From the moment you start until the moment you finish, sex in the real world is awkward and beautiful. Movies (not porn) are pretty much the only place we observe sexual encounters. Those multi-million-dollar budgets with perfect lighting and attractive actors make it look so natural, so effortless, and so breathtaking. You may feel like your relationship is anything but those things, and you would be right. A movie is typically an hour-and-a-half-long work of fiction. You live in the real world; your life is non-fiction. You have a real body and a real spouse who is not reading from a script.
This world wants to dominate the sexual conversation and convince you that you are not having enough fun, and that the real sexy, spontaneous sexual experiences are for

the pop stars and movie icons. Forget them. God has a place of pleasure for you and your spouse. It does have to be cultivated, and that will take work. It will never look like anything you see on a screen. Accept where you are, accept who your spouse is, and begin to develop greater intimacy in your relationship. Let go of what you think it should be like and look forward to an exciting new day.

Lie #3: "My past sex life disqualifies me from a thriving married sex life"
So you made some mistakes? Me too. Human people are imperfect, and that is also true when learning to wield this powerful physical drive for sex, and this even more powerful need for love. No matter the reasons for your indiscretions—how many, how extreme, or how bad you feel—God desires to redeem you from every single one. You do not have to live under the shadow of past relationships. You can choose to let go of what was, forgive yourself, and accept the forgiveness that has been provided to you by God. You can cut every tie from every sexual encounter prior to marriage by asking God to forgive you, cleanse you, heal you, and sanctify you.

Create the Foundation
No matter how long you've been married, or the current state of your sex life, today can be a new day.

1. Identify: What holds you back in your sex life?

Past Experiences

Past Trauma

Fear or Insecurity

Unresolved issues in my marriage

No time, no energy, no prioritization

2. Explore: Areas that need growth and healing

Do I need to make sex and intimacy a forethought, not an afterthought?

Do I need to confess something to my spouse?

Do I need to forgive or be forgiven?

Do I need professional counseling? Do we need professional counseling?

3. Learn: Have learned all I can about sex in marriage?

Have I explored all the Bible says about sex?

What do I need to unlearn?

Am I willing to learn and grow by reading books and blogs?

Am I willing to learn more about giving?

Am I willing to learn more about receiving?

4. Pray: Your sex life belongs in your prayer life

Start praying before every encounter.

Believe God hears you

Believe that this is a prayer He wants to answer

Prayer:
God, I invite you into our intimate relationship. You are the One who created sex, and I pray you would help us have the highest expression of all that you desire in the marriage relationship with and for each other. I pray you would help me to be a loving and giving partner. Help me to completely enjoy the blessing of sex. Amen.

This is my prayer that I chose to pray on my own. Praying is an expression of my faith in God, but also the effort I chose to invest in my sexual relationship. Couples can and should pray together about their intimate life. But in my case, I did not ask, pressure, or expect anything from Ben. The whole premise of my prayer was to give something to him.

The books I recommend:

Dr. Kevin Leman, Sheet Music: Uncovering the Secrets of Sexual Intimacy in Marriage (Tyndale, 2011)

Gary Thomas and Debra K. Fileta, Married Sex, A Christian Couple's Guide to Reimagining Your Love Life (Zondervan, 2021)

Sheila Wray Gregoire, The Good Girl's Guide to Great Sex (And You Thought Bad Girls Had All The Fun) (Zondervan, 2012)

" GOD TAKES OUR DEEPEST NEED FOR LOVE AND OUR PHYSICAL DESIRE FOR SEX AND PRODUCES INTIMACY. TRUE INTIMACY PRODUCES WHOLENESS.

Journal

_____

_____

_____

_____

_____

_____

_____

_____

_____

_____

_____

_____

_____

_____

_____

_____

_____

_____

_____

_____

_____

_____

_____

Week Eight

CHOOSING MARRIAGE VALUES AND LIVING YOUR MARRIAGE MISSION

"**ARTICULATING YOUR VALUES WILL TAKE A LONG TIME, AND YOUR REAL VALUES WILL LAST A LIFETIME. VALUES HELP YOU MAKE DECISIONS ABOUT WHO YOU ARE AND WHERE YOU ARE GOING.**

CHOOSING MARRIAGE VALUES AND LIVING YOUR MARRIAGE MISSION

We all want to be something. I might even go as far to say that we all want to be something more and better than we are today. Like you, I've been on a journey to improve, to grow, to change. But often when I thought I was "growing," I was really just grasping. I was grasping at little bits of wisdom or examples and trying to distill a new lesson down into my heart. I don't know about you, but at times I didn't feel like I made much progress at all. I became frustrated with my lack of growth.

There was a canyon between my aspirations and my reality. While none of us ever fully arrive, exploring my convictions and then defining my personal values has created a much more linear path of growth. Knowing who you are and who you're not keeps you from grasping and helps you start growing.

Who are you going to be? Better, how are you going to become who you want to be?

The goal of this week is to better understand yourself and your spouse, so that you are able to live out your shared values on a shared mission. Knowing a bit about yourself can help you articulate your passion more effectively to your spouse, and they to you. The key is to care more about where "we" are going as a couple, than where "I" am going on my journey. It takes two separate people committed to one set of values to realize the vision.

Who are You?
This was John's testimony when the Jewish leaders sent priests and Temple assistants from Jerusalem to ask John, "Who are you?"
He came right out and said, "I am not the Messiah."
"Well then, who are you?" they asked. "Are you Elijah?"
"No," he replied.
"Are you the Prophet we are expecting?"
"No." (John replied)
 "Then who are you? We need an answer for those who sent us. What do you have to say about yourself?"
John replied in the words of the prophet Isaiah: "I am a voice shouting in the wilderness, 'Clear the way for the Lord's coming!'"

> **Then the Pharisees who had been sent asked him, "If you're not the Messiah or Elijah or the Prophet, what right do you have to baptize?" John told them, "I baptize with water, but right here in the crowd is someone you do not recognize. Though his ministry follows mine, I'm not even worthy to be his slave and untie the straps of his sandal." (John 1:19–27 NLT emphasis the author's)**

John the Baptist teaches us an incredible lesson in choosing values and living our mission. He could state who he was, where his identity came from, and the mission he was on. The Pharisees were asking him to tell them how important he was and if he was famous or had all the answers. John knew he was not the Messiah. or Elijah. Humbly and simply, he stated his part in the story. When asked repeatedly, "Who are you?" He said, "I am a voice shouting in the wilderness, 'Clear the way for the Lord's coming!'" He shows us that his identity came from his relationship with God. The starting point of his existence was oriented around that identity.

John's mission was to baptize with water because this was "how" he would carry out being the voice in the wilderness and clearing the way for the Lord. Our values and mission help us understand our small part in God's big story.

John had a deep level of clarity and security in who he was. That made it easy to stand up to peer pressure, obstacles, and, of course, his own ego. If John were insecure, he might have taken the opportunity to defend himself or appear to be more important than he was. That is often what we do when we lack clarity about who we are. We rush to fill the void and appear bigger and better than we actually are. This only leaves us more confused and scared.

When you know who you are—and you know that God knows you—it doesn't really matter who else knows you, sees you, or validates you.

This world is constantly bombarding you with the questions: "Who are you?" and "What right do you have to be doing what you're doing?"

Do you know the answer? Can you state it?
Can you articulate your marriage values and the mission in your marriage? Or even in life?

Do you have the clarity, security, and humility of John?

Defining your values and mission will foster clarity, security, and humility.

This week exists to help you identify your deep inner convictions or values—specifically regarding your marriage—and then utilize them to write the mission for your marriage. I will share some of my values and mission later.

What are values?

I like to define the term values as my deep inner convictions. They are enduring principles that I live by. They are not necessarily on trend but are classic and never go out of style. These are my non-negotiables that are so deeply a part of who I am that I have difficulty even articulating them. My values have often been felt internally before they were spoken.

After college, my first professional job was with a global recruiting firm in a branch office of five people. I loved my job and the people I worked with. At least two or three times per week, my colleagues invited me out for drinks after work. I don't consume alcohol, so I would often decline their invitation without giving a specific reason. They began to comment and makes jokes about how I never went with them. I had strong convictions regarding alcohol and had no desire to go with them, but I could not verbalize my reasons.

I felt confused and conflicted. Was I judgmental? Did I think I was better than them? Was I reclusive? Was I a goody-two-shoes? Was it my faith or Christian lifestyle? I carried this tumultuous conflict of constantly letting my friends down, while deeply knowing that I could not let myself down. The right words were just outside of my reach.

After agonizing reflection, soul searching, and prayer, it occurred to me one day that my reasons had nothing to do with my feelings about consumption of alcohol or personal choices. Even being a Christian had little to do with my lack of desire to go to the occasional happy hour.

My father was an alcoholic. I would describe him as functional—just barely. My mom was his constant enabler. Without her, he would have easily slipped into a completely non-functional state.

Alcohol represented nothing but pain, poverty, separation, and chaos. I had never observed people drinking in moderation and enjoying normal and productive lives. I finally realized that my deeply held value was that alcohol was not fun. It did not represent joy, conversation, relaxation, and relationships—all things my well-meaning coworkers were hoping to create. For me, it was the exact opposite. And you know what? That's okay. Having that personal awareness addressed my inner conflicts. My newfound clarity gave way to personal security. The negative feelings diminished, and I was able to discuss with my coworkers openly. This took humility. I mean, who wants to tell people stuff like that? But that humility created empathy, and empathy brought about a deeper relationship. Now that I could articulate my value system, they understood. We created a deeper bond than happy hours could ever provide.

Because alcoholism in my family is generational, I have made the decision to never consume it for any reason, at any time. I'm breaking the chain. The story I've shared happened sixteen years ago, and while I've healed from much of my childhood, my value remains the same. No matter how society changes— what's trendy and what's not—this is my personal core value. I'm not changing.

Just like anything else, you have to discover what you believe, why you believe it, and then determine what you should do about it.

Putting Deep Convictions into Words:

Articulating your values will take a long time, and your real values will last a lifetime. Values help you make decisions about who you are and where you are going.

Prior to putting words to my values, I could make decisions but so much was still unclear. Once I was able to articulate why I felt what I felt or did what I did, I was able to steer my life where I wanted to ultimately go.

Your values and identity come from somewhere.

The question is where? I've found my values have come from two places:
1. The wisdom found in God's word, first and foremost
2. Observing life, both positive and negative

My deeply held values have usually stemmed from a problem I have observed in life and the solution I have found in the scripture.

Why do Values Matter?

Values inform actions, actions over time create habits, and habits create a life.
Values—not feelings—define my standards.
Feelings are fleeting. Values are permanent. The stability we seek is often found in the values we live by.

Here is an example:
I have a personal core value around kindness. My articulated value is: "Treat others with the highest level of kindness and respect."

That came from:

Problem observed in life:
I was bullied, criticized, and, at times, humiliated. Watching others be bullied, criticized, and humiliated left a deep impression on me to never make someone feel how I have felt.

Solution I've found in the scripture:
When others weren't kind, Jesus was.

"In his kindness God called you to share in his eternal glory by means of Christ Jesus. So after you have suffered a little while, he will restore, support, and strengthen you, and he will place you on a firm foundation."
(1 Peter 5:10 NLT)

The combination of the scripture and my observations affects me today. I have a visceral reaction to people being embarrassed and treated poorly, especially in front of others. Every person deserves to be treated with the highest level of kindness and respect. Am I perfect? Definitely not. But you will never hear me speak ill of someone else behind their back. Does my lack of perfection negate my core value? No way.

Core values speak to who you already are, and core values are transformational:

1. I am not perfectly kind. Life informed me of what I do not want to be. The scripture transformed me into who I want to become.

2. I do not drink alcohol, but I have struggled with other excessive patterns in my life

at times—like eating or spending. I aspire to be moderate and disciplined in every area of my life by the power of Christ, with my mind renewed according to the scripture.

Your Values in Your Marriage

So, what does any of this have to do with my marriage? How is this helping me choose my spouse more effectively?

And will this help my marriage thrive?

I bet you have observed some situations in marriages that you never want to see repeated. You might know what the scripture says about marriage, and you aspire to model your marriage after the scripture. No matter what your deep inner convictions are and whether they were birthed from pain or joy, articulating them is one of the most powerful things you can do.

Here is one of my marriage values from scripture:

"A wise woman builds her house, but the foolish woman pulls it down with her own hands." (Proverbs 14:1 NKJV emphasis the author's)

I observed women who have done a beautiful job building, those who have tragically destroyed their houses, and those who seem to build with one hand and tear down with another. At times, I've been all of those.

I have chosen to be a builder with my actions, my words, and my attitudes. In everything I do, I try to be building up, encouraging, and growing my husband and my family. I often pray this scripture over myself and use it as a roadmap for my behavior.

Why? And what difference might this make?

Much of marriage is invisible to the eye. Often, we measure the quality of the marriage by the smiles we see or the happiness we feel. Whether we realize it or not, a marriage creates a legacy of examples, lessons, experiences, and memories, in addition to sharing life with another human.

The legacy we are creating can be positive or negative at the end of our life. We can build or destroy—it's rarely neutral. The reason for my value is to strategically build the invisible parts of my marriage, such as:

1. An example of loyalty
2. My husband's confidence
3. My children's view of marriage and healthy family dynamics
4. A deep foundation of trust

Let's put some words to our marriage values:

Here are some value-based ideas to consider
1. A value regarding unity could look like never saying the word divorce, or only using words that strengthen your bond. Read about unity in Psalm 133:1-3 & 1 Corinthians 1:10.
2. A value about being a trustworthy, loyal, and loving spouse can be found in Proverbs 31.
3. A value about intimacy can be found in the Song of Solomon.
4. A value about the type of spouse you will be is in Proverbs 12:4.

You can create values around all areas of life:
1. Discipleship and Walking with God
2. Parenting
3. Stewardship and Finances
4. Goals and Success
5. Lifestyle Habits / Physical Health

Take some time to write down your marriage convictions, and then craft statements that you can speak over your life and your marriage:

_____

_____

_____

_____

Values are the car, and Mission is the map.
Values are who I am, the Mission is what I consistently do with who I am.
So, where are we going?

Mission

Now that you know your values and understand your deep personal convictions, where will they take you?

The real power is discovered when the values and mission work in conjunction to help you arrive at the desired destination that honors God and builds a legacy worth following.

Values and Mission Example:

Value: "I am a wise woman building my house which includes my spouse and my children." - Proverbs 14:1

Mission: Every day, I will make wise choices that build my family up in their confidence, spiritual walk with God, loyalty, and integrity. I do this through prayer, transformation by reading God's word, my choices, and my example. I am building a shelter of love for my family to abide within. No matter what I feel like, this is my mission. I will rid myself and my house of destructive tendencies like strife, division, insecurity, disorganization, and confusion.

Value and Mission Exercise:

1. Value: _____

2. Mission: _____

1. Value: _____

2. Mission: _____

1. Value: _____

2. Mission: _____

Live your life through the filter of your values and do everything possible to live out your mission. Over time, you begin to see that you are building something strong and beautiful that stands the test of time.

Journal

TWENTY FIVE WAYS TO CHOOSE YOUR SPOUSE

1. Stop the argument as soon as it starts.

2. Plan an entire date, start to finish, including babysitting.

3. Cook their favorite meal.

4. Make plans for their favorite type of recreation.

5. Send an encouraging text.

6. Do one thing today that you know matters to them.

7. Find a way to celebrate them in front of other people.

8. Buy them a small gift and leave it where they can find it.

9. Put a husband or wife appreciation post on social media.

10. Stock up on their favorite drinks or snacks.

11. Frame their favorite family pictures for their desk.

12. When life is against them, be their voice of unflinching support.

13. Listen intently, looking into their eyes.

14. Create opportunities for your family to laugh.

15. Kiss for thirty seconds.

16. Hug four to six times per day.

17. Don't ignore any requests for something to change.

18. Say "thank you" often.

19. Pray for your spouse.

20. Prank them.

21. Hold hands more often.

22. Tell them how grateful you are that they married you.

23. Initiate sex.

24. Watch what they want to watch (at least once).

25. Set goals together for the upcoming year.

POST STUDY RESOURCES:

SCRIPTURE AND PRAYERS FOR YOUR MARRIAGE TO THRIVE AND HEAL

A Prayer for Starting Your Marriage Well
Reading: Genesis 2:23

God, thank You for this incredible gift of marriage. I pray that you help me treat my spouse with all the love and respect that I desire for myself. I pray that you give me the wisdom to invest in my spouse continually. May I have the eyes to clearly see their needs and a heart to respond to their desires.

In Jesus Name, Amen.

A Prayer for Building Your Marriage and Family
Reading: Proverbs 14:1

God, I pray that I am a wise woman who builds my house. I desire to build my husband, my family, myself, and my relationship with You. I will build with my words, my actions, and my attitudes. Reveal the areas where I am consistently pulling down my spouse, myself, and my family, creating frustration and pain with my own hands. I pray that I build an atmosphere to nurture, care for, and build my family up in You.

In Jesus Name, Amen.

A Prayer for A Marriage that Seems Impossible to Fix
Reading: Ezekiel 37:1–14

"And He said to me, 'Son of man, can these bones live?' So I answered, 'O Lord God, You know.'" (v. 3 emphasis the author's)

God, you know that my marriage is like the valley of dry bones. Utterly dry, and void of love and life. Today, I speak to my marriage and the dry places of my own heart. I believe you can, and ask You to do a powerful miracle in my marriage—taking us from death to life. I will take you at Your word, speak life over my marriage, and take up my part to see Your promise come to pass.

In Jesus Name, Amen.

A Prayer to Foster Unity
Reading: Psalm 133:1–3, Philippians 2:1–4

God, I pray that my spouse and I would live in total unity and that unity would be pleasing to you and a testimony to others. I pray that you would help me choose to be the agent of unity, always seeking reconciliation and peace. I thank you for the blessing You promised us by choosing unity. I pray that it would cover our house today and for generations to come.

In Jesus Name, Amen.

A Prayer for Greater Intimacy
Reading: Song of Solomon

God, I pray that our marriage would thrive in the area of sexual, emotional, and spiritual intimacy. I bring my past to you—my baggage and the unhealed parts of who I am—and I ask You to do a great work in me and in my spouse. We desire the fullest expression that you have for a married couple. I surrender all to You and thank You for the gift of sex.

In Jesus Name, Amen.

A Prayer for a Spouse Who Is Not Walking with God
Reading: 2 Corinthians 7:16
God, I lift up my spouse to You, as I have many times before. I pray that their heart would turn toward you and that You would send people into their life to remind them of just how good You are. Help me to be an example of Your love, grace, mercy, and kindness. My deepest desire is that one day we would serve you together, worship in church together, and be a spiritual example together.

In Jesus Name, Amen.

A Prayer While Walking through Betrayal and Heartbreak
Reading: Psalm 34:18, Psalm 147:3

God, I pray that You would heal my broken heart and my crushed spirit, and that somehow You would help us rebuild trust, communication, and unity. We need a miracle that only You can provide. Every day, I will lean on You to be my support and my strength. Heal my mind from the trauma. Heal my spirit from the wounds. I ask that You would give us a new beginning.

In Jesus Name, Amen.

INDEX

COPYRIGHT PAGE

CPSIA information can be obtained
at www.ICGtesting.com
Printed in the USA
LVHW070559310323
742779LV00002B/8